T0316154

20/20 Hindsight

From Starting Up to Successful Entrepreneur, By Those Who've Been There

Rachelle Thackray

First published in Great Britain in 2002 by
Virgin Books Ltd
Thames Wharf Studios
Rainville Road
London
W6 9HA

ISBN 0 7535 0547 9

Series Consultant: Professor David Storey
Joint Series Editors: Robert Craven, Grier Palmer

Whilst care has been taken in the preparation of this book, no responsibility for
any loss occasioned to any person acting or refraining from any action as a result
of any material in this publication can be accepted by the author or publisher or
anyone connected with the series. Views expressed in this publication are not
necessarily those of Warwick Business School or the University of Warwick.

Series design by Janice Mather at Ben Cracknell Studios
Typeset by Phoenix Photosetting, Chatham, Kent

Printed and bound in Great Britain by Clays Ltd, St Ives PLC

Contents

Acknowledgements

My thanks go to Tess Poole; to the *Independent*, which published many initial conversations in its business review pages in the series Me & My Partner and My Biggest Mistake; to all the entrepreneurs who have kindly taken time to contribute to this book; and to my parents and Andy.

Disclaimer

All interviews were carried out between 1999 and 2001 and all information was correct, as far as could be verified, at the time of going to press. Some quotes have been slightly modified to improve the sense or flow of the narrative.

Foreword to the Series
by Sir Richard Branson

It feels a bit odd to be writing a foreword to a business book. Perhaps it's because I haven't always done business by the book myself. Sometimes I've regretted that, and sometimes I've been glad that I followed my instincts instead of doing what conventional advisers might have recommended.

One thing I've learned is that there's no right way to do things in life. There is no 'magic bullet' for success in business. What works for Virgin Atlantic might not be right for British Airways; what suits your business could be completely wrong for someone else's. But any advice that can help you beat the odds and succeed in business has got to be a good thing. Listening to lots of people's ideas before taking a decision has always been something I have strongly believed in.

Every book in this series has been written by an expert in his or her field, and they've come up with lots of interesting and thought-provoking ideas. But the most important thing is to do what you personally feel is right.

Business should be fun. Enjoy what you do, and success comes within reach.

Good luck!

Preface

This book describes in a structured way the four key steps in developing a business: the ideas underlying it, preparing to start it, getting it started and keeping it going.

While this structure is quite conventional, what makes the book come alive is that the text reflects the author's conversations with more than 150 owners or part-owners of businesses. All of these owners not only have an informative short biography in the Who's Who at the end, but they also have their remarks attributed to them within the text.

The entrepreneurs themselves are a fascinating bunch of people who broadly reflect the types of businesses being established by people nowadays. Many are in the media, publishing and financial services sectors but, like any collection of small businesses, they exhibit considerable diversity: they range from one that makes shaving products, to another that is now a leading producer of computer mouse mats.

The entrepreneurs, as individuals, also show why making generalisations about small business owners is so difficult. Quite a number of them have been educated at the UK's leading universities, yet they also include individuals suffering severe dyslexia and many with virtually no educational qualifications at all.

Rachelle Thackray then blends conversations with these individuals into ten chapters, getting them to look back and distil their business experience. The author then highlights a set of questions, the replies to which constitute a summary of experience.

The reader is then encouraged to answer a set of questions about their own business ideas, providing answers in fewer than ten words.

I certainly recommend this book to any individual contemplating starting a business, but also to those acting as business advisers. In my judgement the combination of careful structuring, but using a conversational format, is a business winner.

Professor David Storey
Director, Centre for Small and Medium Sized Enterprises
Warwick Business School, University of Warwick

If you have ever dreamed of starting up a business, you may have wondered how successful entrepreneurs started from scratch. What were their first steps? What experience and aptitude did they possess naturally, and how much did they learn on the job? Can ordinary people set up companies – and does that make them entrepreneurs? What determines whether a business succeeds and makes a profit, or fails and goes bust? What kinds of pressures are involved in starting up a business? At what point do expectations meet reality?

Entrepreneurs are commonly perceived to possess youth, charm, ambition, drive, ruthlessness, energy, the ability to spot an opportunity and the willingness to take a risk. Do you really need all these qualities and, even then, are they sufficient? Any seasoned entrepreneur will tell you that the best teacher is experience. Starting a business is invariably a pressurised, intense and unpredictable procedure and the single most important trait for success is probably sheer persistence or resilience – the ability to keep going in the face of failure and learn from mistakes.

Some of the world's best businesses start in back bedrooms based solely on a dream and fuelled by extraordinary amounts of determination and drive. Countless other businesses, fuelled by similar amounts of energy and enthusiasm, never make it out of the bedroom, collapsing after months of struggle. What makes the difference between the two? Luck? Timing? Or other factors? What enables an initial idea to grow into a sizeable organisation?

Many companies in this book have moved beyond start-up into new stages of development, yet they remain cautious about calling themselves 'successful'. Success is relative and comes in all shades, though profit is obviously key for any business to survive and grow. Some companies grow rapidly without a hitch, while others judge their achievement more in terms of managing to stay afloat through turbulent times. One entrepreneur pointed out that 20/20 foresight was just as important, if not more so, than learning from hindsight. Nevertheless I hope that this book, with its collection of diverse experiences, will be a useful primer for anyone who has always dreamed of starting a business and wants to know more about how to do it.

PART ONE

FROM IDEA TO EXECUTION

Chapter One

This chapter looks at why people start up businesses. Being an entrepreneur is not a job that suits everyone, but it does have the peculiar distinction of being an occupation open to all comers. Are some more likely than others to become entrepreneurs? What motivates them? What makes for success?

In the genes

For some people, business runs in the blood. Early experiences of enterprise, although not the sole determining factor, can help mark out the course for an entrepreneurial career. As a child, **Mike Altendorf** loved to talk with his grandfather, an Austrian Jew who fled Europe during wartime to become a dishwasher in New York and went on to establish a chain of supermarkets in the States. 'My grandfather had great ideas about how to sell stuff,' he says. 'He once built a blueberry mountain with a sign saying, BLUEBERRIES ON OFFER, LIMITED TO TWO TINS PER PERSON – and, of course, everybody went berserk and had to have them.'

Barrie Pearson started his corporate finance boutique after working for large companies and, like many others, recalls entrepreneurial tendencies as a child. 'My father loved gardening and every year he would grow a garden full of flowers. At the age of seven I persuaded him to let me cut them and sell them by knocking on people's doors – and I put my sister in charge of selling from our home by putting a sign out because we lived on a main road. At the age of eight, I persuaded my father to grow vegetables and I sold them to a nearby wholesaler.'

For **Jeremy Seigal**, running stalls at charity fêtes was an early experience of doing business. 'Things are only worth what someone else is prepared to pay,' he says, 'and, as a shopkeeper, you can never have enough change.'

The two women who founded The Curtain Exchange say they learned enterprise from their parents. 'My mother ran her own business for forty years,' explains **Juliana Galvin**, 'so I had experience of what it was to be self-employed and a certain confidence that you didn't have to look to anyone else for a wage.'

Andrew Lindsay saw his father run several businesses in the seventies and eighties, including a restaurant and an office-cleaning business. 'My dad and I were quite competitive,' he says, 'so perhaps it was in my genes to say to myself, You've got to get out there, son.'

> **20/20** . . . 'We've had several "once in a lifetime" opportunities. You tend to get good luck and bad luck in equal measures. But you're really fortunate if you get the good luck when you can take advantage of it and the bad luck when it doesn't matter.'
> – William Harris

As children, **Alex** and **Nicko van Someren** helped their father run his business from home. 'It helped to have been brought up in an entrepreneurial family where my father showed me that it was OK to work for yourself and that you didn't need other people's permission to have a job,' says Alex. 'It is extremely important to have the environmental support. Lots of people have parents who say, "You've got to go to university," whereas I was given a completely different social education by my family.'

Daniel Gestetner expected to succeed to the family photocopier business, but his father sold the business to an Australian conglomerate when he was in his late teens. 'Not having that opportunity was a big challenge for me,' he says. 'I had always felt I could run a business but first my father said, "Go and make some mistakes." I spoke to some of his business friends and the resounding advice was, "Learn from someone else."' Gestetner then worked for Tesco and Revlon before starting his own venture in the late nineties.

For others there is no family support at all – and this may intensify the determination to succeed. **William Sargent** became an entrepreneur against his father's wishes. 'My father wasn't a risk taker because he was a chartered accountant. He was very clever and made a lot of money for other people, but never followed his own advice. I went to the other extreme – I have been an entrepreneur since I was eighteen, which made my father very uneasy. I borrowed my first £100 from the bank to buy some disco turntables, and he wouldn't guarantee it, but I badgered the bank manager and paid it back in three weeks.'

> **20/20** . . . 'People who know anything about it probably don't start businesses because they know what they are letting themselves in for.'
>
> – John Mortimer

Karen Haddon left stage school to go into show business but soon joined her father's fireworks business and found new ways to develop her creative talents. 'I was intrigued to watch my father and learned a lot very quickly by listening to him doing deals and observing his business acumen,' she says. 'I found it fascinating and tried to emulate him. I began to feel very comfortable in that environment.'

Graham Cherry joined his father's business, Countryside Properties, as a graduate trainee, and is now its chief executive. 'I remember being a long way ahead of my colleagues at university in terms of business sense and enterprise,' he says. 'My father brought us up and we lived together through the property crash of the mid-seventies. Cash management was drilled into us at a very young age. We have always had this very disciplined approach: maximising the return is something we've always been very conscious of. We were brought up with an ethic of hard work. Sometimes the children of successful people drift and become lazy; my brother and I were the opposite.'

As a teenager, **Jack Morris** had ideas of being a theatre impresario, but his father had other plans for him. 'Business was always part of our culture when we were young,' explains Morris. 'When we were kids we used to come into the office during our holidays and answer the phone or do the photocopying. We assimilated the culture and we always took an interest in what my dad was up to. We all had Saturday jobs from the age of sixteen onwards.

'Our family culture was that we earned our wages – we didn't get pocket money and we learned the value of a few quid. When I finished at school, I went to a further-education college but was ready to go to work. My father sat me down and asked me what I was going to do and I said, "I'm not really sure," and he said, "Look, I've got four boys in the business who work in production or sales. The area we really need to cover is a skill in finance." Understanding the figures, as he put it.'

Morris was reluctant to join the family firm at first. 'I hated maths, it was boring, but Dad said, "Look, do me a favour. Why don't you go and work for our accountants for six months? If you don't like it, fine, we'll talk again."

'You can't argue with the logic of that. I ended up staying for four or five years because I realised that there was going to be a niche for me in the business, so I stuck it out.'

He also learned the 'trade' of an entrepreneur from his father: 'My dad came from a very poor East End background, a huge family of nine kids. As soon as they could leave school, at fourteen, they would go out to bring money in. My dad went to work at Billingsgate fish market and had that work ethic. He was also a great opportunist – he could spot an opportunity and capitalise upon it; he could look at a situation and know that an opportunity would arise.

'I learned a lot from him about tenacity. He was a guy who would hang on to something and not let it go, like a dog with a bone. He was also a very good people person, listening and working out what made them tick. To me, measuring the person you are doing business with is the beginning of everything. You can look at a deal and it might be wonderful, but, if there isn't going to be the chemistry, you don't ever get to second base. A lot of what I've done, I learned at my father's knee. He mentored me because I had this training in finance and he saw me as a safe pair of hands.'

20/20 . . . 'By all means start your business just as soon as possible. Don't procrastinate but do make sure you have researched your market, developed your business model and have ample finance available first.'

– Barrie Pearson

Next step

James Keay wanted his own business even from the age of six or seven. 'I was the kid with three paper rounds instead of one, and at school I had an illegal tuck shop making £60 a week. When I got caught, I offered to give the school 50 per cent of the profits but they told me my time would be better spent elsewhere.'

Richard Thwaite dreamed of having his own business from an early age and did a management degree 'as a stepping stone' before entering a graduate sales scheme, where 'every time you were on a deal, you were working very much like a small business or franchise'. He adds, 'A career as an entrepreneur was always going to be the way forward for me. My vision and ideas, combined with the desire to bring these to fruition, meant that working for someone else was an unattractive proposition. Put simply, I love working in a team, as long as I'm the captain.'

Neil Franklin began in business in his late teens. 'When I was younger I used to flick through the *Yellow Pages* for ideas and pick out the companies with the biggest adverts because I thought they must be the most successful. If I went into somewhere, a bar or shop, I'd ask, "What would I do differently?" Then, in college, a guy said to me, "Do you want to earn some extra money?" So I began working door to door for a wall-coating company. Then I realised I could set up in business by asking each house owner what they wanted and sell those leads as business information. Each lead was worth £25, so I could earn £100 by talking to a house owner for ten minutes and saying, "What home improvements are you considering?" '

Mark Dixon also points to early formative experiences. 'I organised discos for my scout group while I was at school, and I had a multitude of jobs during my early teenage years. Through these, I gained an enormous amount of experience – both for organising these small enterprises and also working with a variety of people as they operated their businesses – and this taught me the value of hard work and focus. Of all the people I worked with, the ones who succeeded were the ones who were really focused on the business and who relentlessly worked on the detail in order to improve the model.'

Finding a mentor or getting good training at an early stage is of real benefit to an entrepreneur, says **Aziz Cami**. 'One thing I regret is that I didn't work for better people prior to going into business. When we founded The Partners, we were doing OK but we didn't really have the quality threshold that I would have been proud of. You can shape your career from a very early start by being quite rigorous about who you work for. You can accelerate your development and learn so much from good people and I think if you're very astute, and looking to learn and develop, you have to be quite ruthless about who you work for. That gives you confidence to make a move early.'

> **20/20** . . . 'If you are starting with nothing, you haven't got a lot to lose by setting up on your own.'
> – Terry Pullen

Richard Reed says it took some years to put his plans for his own business into action. At eleven, he was doodling names for imaginary companies on his school textbooks, and at fourteen he started a gardening business. Then, after college, he took a job at an advertising agency. 'Four years into my career, I remembered, "I thought you wanted to start your own business?" I sat in a meeting and thought, "In five years' time I'm going to be sitting in a very similar meeting doing very similar things. I'm not sure if I want to have it work out like that." From that point on, it was a little bit of a thorn in my side.'

His friend and partner **Jon Wright** says, 'It got to the point where we either had to put our heads down and make a career, or say, "We're twenty-seven, we don't have mortgages or kids – now's a great time to try those things we've always wanted to do."'

After spending several years as a social worker, **Charlotte Barker** began to think about developing further a board game that she had designed at college. 'I felt quite institutionalised. I was spending time empowering other people and helping them talk about their lives and their dreams, but had lost that in myself. When I graduated and took my first job, I put the game into a cupboard for ten years. I never thought about it again till 1998, when I had lost my way. My partner reminded me, "You've got a game in the cupboard. Why don't you get that out?" I had two weeks' holiday, so I sat at the kitchen table and got on with [developing] it.'

Control

Successful entrepreneurs who have never worked for anyone, say creative and financial freedom are key motivators, as well as benefits. According to **Simon Needham**, 'I've never been offered the chance to work for another company but the thought of having a boss – no, it frightens me to think about that. I don't mind working as equals, sitting around a board table. That's cool and you end up coming up with better conclusions. But someone saying, "Do this, do that" – my passion would disappear.'

Simon Notley became an entrepreneur 'probably from the desire not to work for anybody else and the realisation that working for somebody else, financially, is fairly restrictive. The opportunities aren't there, however good you might get.' And for **Jeremy Seigal**, 'creating wealth gives me a real buzz as I can see the results of my efforts'.

> **20/20 . . .** 'We have always wanted to become very wealthy people. We're both very ambitious to make a lot of money. You need that burning desire.'
>
> – Graham Cherry

Adam Twiss decided to set up his own software company after spending a summer working for a large corporation in 1994. 'It was everything that could be wrong with an IT company: it had great technology in the seventies and a huge market share but the attitude when I worked there was completely "can't do". I remember we came back from a company presentation and I was asking my boss, "Why don't we develop this software ourselves?" And he said, "We're not big enough to develop software any more." So I thought, hang on, we're the biggest computer company in Europe and we're buying this software from a company one-hundredth of our size. Starting Zeus was about wanting to prove a point, show what was possible and make more of a difference.'

> **20/20** . . . 'All I knew was that I didn't want to work for anyone, because I'm a rebellious bastard. I had nothing to lose by going into business, is the simple truth of it.'
>
> – Martin Rutty

Numerous entrepreneurs tell how they began their careers in large organisations, rose to become leaders, became frustrated with corporate structures and, when control was taken away, left to start up something new.

Nick Austin started out as a salesman at Procter & Gamble, but says, 'What I couldn't stand was this sense of straitjacket – that you must not under any circumstances break the rules. I'm a bit of a rebel and a nonconformist and I always kicked back against big business and big organisations.

'One reason why I flowered in my twenties was that I found myself in an unstructured company, Matchbox, which had just come through a difficult period. There was no depth of management and we were pretty much allowed to do what we wanted as long as we could make the numbers work. It was the perfect environment – [and] a bit like taking the stabilisers off a bike. You realise you can do it and, the more you do it, the better you get.'

Austin then persuaded his boss at Matchbox to let him try to turn the ailing company around. 'I was twenty-nine and European marketing manager, but I desperately wanted the job of managing director and they were going to put it out to a headhunter. I picked up the phone to my boss and said, "Why are you phoning a head-hunter when you haven't asked me to do the job?" He said, "In two or three years' time, you'll be great. But I can't ask you to run this, because you haven't got the experience." I said, "That's not fair. I've got more experience and understanding than anyone you could bring in. Give me a year to prove it."'

Austin got the job. In the end, he and the finance director, **Alan Bennie,** were so successful that Matchbox was sold to a larger group and they left to start up their own toy company, Vivid Imaginations.

Nicola Murphy and **Jessica Hatfield** each recall a turning point that led to them founding their own companies. Murphy says, 'I went out with my boss and his associates, and ended up having one drink too many and telling him how to run his business. I wasn't very polite, and I woke up the next morning and thought I'd get sacked. I even rang a client and said I thought I'd get the sack, and this client asked, "Would that be such a bad thing? Perhaps you should consider running your own business." '

Hatfield worked for a large firm and 'assumed that if someone held a superior position to [her], they automatically knew what they were doing'. The moment of revelation came when she presented a strategy she had developed to the board of the company she was working for. 'I had a very clear picture of where I wanted to go and the board was receptive until the marketing director stood up and said, "She means well, but I don't think she understands what she's doing." That moment gave me the courage to leave. I knew without a shadow of a doubt that I was right and he was wrong, so I left the company to set up on my own. Once I'd broken through my own glass ceiling, there was nothing I couldn't do.'

Jon Moulton ran Schroder Ventures for eight years but left when he felt it became restrictive. 'I built things up from myself and a secretary to a huge business . . . but Schroder wanted their ball back.' He went to work for another firm but was irritated by 'lots of meetings and discussions', so, in 1997, he set up his own firm, Alchemy Partners. 'I had been pretty successful in large organisations and piled up enough cash to be able to say, "I will set up because I can afford failure." It was far easier than I thought – I was well known in the venture trade. I thought it would take longer to get the team and the money together.'

> **20/20** . . . 'Neither of us liked politics . . . [or] millions of meetings with professional meeting-goers.'
> – Phil Docker

Sharon Reed worked her way up from being a secretary to managing a subsidiary within a large communications group. 'I suppose I was a bit of a pain – I carved out territory for myself, grabbed anything that looked interesting and eventually got sent on a management course. I began ringing people and making appointments and was rewarded by seeing this subsidiary begin to make a profit.'

She left in the mid-eighties to set up FrameStore. 'A new boss was brought in who didn't give me the equality that I asked for. One or two people said, "Why don't you set your own business up?" As a teenager I was good at a lot of things but never fantastic at one thing, and I'd always felt I would be good at running a business.'

Sue Welland resigned from her corporate job after being cut out of the loop. 'I discovered that a number of my staff had been taken off the email system before I arrived at work. There hadn't been any discussion about it. I thought, "I've had it with corporate life – it's not about empowerment, there's not enough control and I'm working for other people's values." I felt the things I wanted to do weren't anything to do with somebody giving me their approval.'

20/20 . . . 'I didn't like being told off for my mistakes. Nobody gives you a bigger bollocking than yourself. It's only when you start to work for yourself that you really learn.'

– Paul Varcoe

Asked to merge with another business, **David Abraham** and **Andy Law** took the team they had built and started up a new advertising agency, St Luke's. 'The story begins with me and Andy being employees of a progressive but independent American advertising agency,' says Abraham. 'There was always a sense of being part of something international but also we were independent in London. All that was jeopardised when the founder wanted to retire and get out of advertising. He sold the agency and we felt strongly that the spirit of what we were trying to do was gone. We were being asked to be part of a big conglomerate and they were trying to merge us with another agency and get rid of staff.' The pair decided to go their own way and set up St Luke's.

'We had had the privilege of experimenting with new ways of working flexibly and looking at progressive ownership structures . . . [but] a lot of ideas we were coming up with were parked. When this happened, Andy and I literally dusted off the documents and said, "If we're going to do this, maybe there are some ideas that we can use." There was a sense of experimentation – the feeling that "the world doesn't need another agency so we'd better make sure we are very different". The drive was to be as radical as we possibly could.'

For some people, it's not a sudden crisis that precipitates change but a process of disenchantment. **Mark Smith** and **Tim Connolly** left their corporate jobs more for professional than entrepreneurial reasons. 'It was beginning to get frustrating, being part of a large corporation, and it took a long time to get anything done. We were treated like adults in the outside world but inside, we were like cogs in a wheel,' says Smith. 'I don't think we actually realised how frustrating that was until it wasn't around us any more. We were also getting uncomfortable with the direction that the big firms were taking.'

Robin Hutson felt a sense of vulnerability. He'd worked in the hotel industry for several years and began to think about running his own place. 'You hear stories of people who work for twenty years for one company and then are made redundant, and I started to think about that. I thought, "I've got to do my own thing. I don't want to work on a salary, essentially at someone else's whim till I'm sixty-five years old." The problem is that you get rather comfortable in your career, and I had two sons both at private schools and a nice house, which all required a certain amount of cash to maintain. I had no family money to use on a project, so the prospect of setting up and then launching myself into the black hole was a slightly hairy one.'

> **20/20** . . . 'We both felt we would rather control our own destinies directly than be in the hands of others making decisions about us.'
>
> – Malcolm Chilton

When **Robyn Jones** was made redundant from her job as a senior catering executive in the early nineties, she decided to take control of her working life by starting her own catering business. 'Being made redundant was a funny time. You can see the practicalities but it still knocks your confidence. I went for interviews to competitors but was asking myself, "Do I want to be an area manager? Do I want to go into sales?"

'I just couldn't get excited about any of these jobs. I suppose I wasn't really selling myself either. I didn't think, "Right, I'm going to set up something," because I didn't have the confidence to be able to do that. Then my husband said, "Maybe now is the time to set up on your own." He gave me the encouragement and said, "Come on, you can do it." Once I'd worked out what I was going to do, energy was not a problem. It was make or break for me, really.'

Getting the habit

Successful entrepreneurs say failure provides a chance to learn. **Richard Thwaite** thought it 'a great shame but a great opportunity' when the computer systems firm he worked for went bust. 'The only logical thing was to start again, but by then Mike [Altendorf] and I had realised there was more money in services and brains than in selling bits of tin. There was a distinct difference between techies and businesspeople and this gave rise to the high-growth sector that embraced new ideas and opinions. The newness of the industry gave people the opportunity to shape it, instead of the industry shaping them.'

Arthur Allen also went into business for himself after the collapse of businesses he worked for. 'I don't think Arthur started to think about doing something on his own until the second company he worked for went bust,' says **Irene Allen**, co-founder of Listawood. 'We didn't see many other options than to do something ourselves. I'd worked in university research labs and going back to work would have meant long periods spent travelling. With our own thing, we felt we had nothing to lose – we just thought, "What the hell, why not?" If it did go wrong, we were fairly confident we could get other jobs.'

An entrepreneur is commonly defined as a risk taker and opportunist, but success most often comes through persistence. **Simon Notley** had been on the verge of bankruptcy and his wife Anne was training to be a solicitor to offset 'the vagaries of running our own businesses over several years'. Despite this, the couple sold their house to finance a new venture, making and selling iron beds. 'The only collateral we had was in our house, which we'd had for ten years,' explains Anne. 'It was a hell of a commitment to sell it . . . but we did it because we could see an opening in the market.'

A disastrous experience of putting on a musical in the West End left **Jon Thoday** with no other option than to continue on his entrepreneurial trajectory. 'At college I set up a theatre company and that taught me how to lose money, as did the show I put on in the West End, *Nightclub Confidential*, which lost more than £400,000. It took two years to get the money together, and about three weeks to lose it. It was an unmitigated disaster. The show had sponsors, but I owed so much personally – £40,000 – that I didn't have any choice but to carry on. I couldn't think of any job which would pay back my overdraft, so, three weeks after the show, I started going round the comedy clubs because it had seemed to me that there was a gap in the market to manage comedians in the same way as bands.'

QUESTIONS FROM THE EDGE

When starting a business, does my age make a difference?

Aziz Cami: 'I started my business in my late twenties, a stage at which I think you tend to be positive and haven't got a lot to lose. In our case, all I could see was the upside. I think it's harder to take that decision the later you get in your life.'

Nick Rose: 'If you make mistakes when you're young, the stakes aren't quite so high and it means that, for future businesses, you will have eradicated some important ones. Our age makes us that much closer to our users; I suppose it also gives us more scope to impress. Being young probably makes us a nightmare to work with in some cases, because we won't take no for an answer.'

Nick Austin: 'I believe it was right when it happened. One of the reasons I didn't become an entrepreneur until I was in my thirties is that I went through the first twenty-five years of my life thinking I wasn't any good at stuff. I failed the eleven-plus, was a very basic academic achiever, and it was only when I did a business studies degree that I clicked into gear. Between the ages of twenty-nine and thirty-five, I ran someone else's business, but the parent company was so hands-off it was almost like running my own. In those six years, we learned so much about how to run an efficient company.'

Howard Leigh: 'You've got to be of an age when you're happy to make the jump. The ideal time is late twenties, early thirties, when you haven't got commitments and you have the energy and you are not worried about things.'

What kind of person should I be to start my own business?

Terry Pullen: 'I've read numerous definitions of what it means to be an entrepreneur. In my view, there's only one thing that

---

sums it up. An entrepreneur is someone who believes they can do it better than other people. It doesn't mean they're any good at anything.'

Anna Russell: 'Some people are predisposed to be entrepreneurial and tend not to be bound by fear as much as the rest of us. I wouldn't say I was a natural entrepreneur. For me, becoming an entrepreneur was more to do with believing in an idea, knowing the market and believing that I could make that idea work well in the marketplace, and really having the confidence and the guts to put everything behind that.'

Charlie Muirhead: 'If there's any single thing that defines an entrepreneur, it's that you become absolutely obsessed and totally persistent about seeing what you want to do either come to reality, or not work. It's persistence that pays off: going back to the drawing board saying, "What didn't work? Is there nothing here or do we need to rethink?" The second thing is leadership. You have to have strong leadership qualities.'

What kind of person should *not* start a business?

Brian Clivaz: 'Some people would not enjoy the lack of security which working for your own company allows you. As an entrepreneur you rely to a much greater extent on your own initiative, enthusiasm and energy. This can mean working for long periods of time without the usual benefits of weekends off and holidays. However, on the positive side you are to a very great degree master of your own destiny and have only yourself to blame if you find yourself in a difficult situation.

'The important thing is to understand that life is a game that you cannot always win. Sometimes you go through long periods of turmoil and even if you lose everything, you have to have the courage and energy to start again. When it all works you are in the enviable position of seemingly having it all, as apart from your investors there is no one who can tell you what to do or how to do it. This gives you a tremendous feeling of freedom, but confidence in yourself and in your vision for the future is the most important defining factor.'

Neil Franklin: 'If you want to look at whether or not you're going to be successful in business, you could probably start with your attitude to life in the present day. If you've got a history of quitting things, don't bother going into business. The person who continually moans that this and that doesn't work, who has a problem enjoying what he or she does and doesn't have a streak of "let's have a go", who is not used to succeeding and will use failure as a reason not to do something – that person should not be in business. Say to your friends, "Am I a committed person?" If they say no, that tells you not to go into business.'

What traits help an entrepreneur to succeed?

Mark Constantine: 'People now say how successful we are, yet it doesn't feel successful and I think that's the personality trait of an entrepreneur. Once you start to feel successful, you have just lost it.'

Sue Welland: 'I think you have to be brave because the worst that can happen is that you can fail. It's not such a big thing. Talk to other people that have done it and get loads of advice from them, which you can choose to ignore if you want to.'

Anna Russell: 'You have to be gutsy in dealing with sceptics. We went out and pitched to different people within the industry, a lot of whom were incredibly supportive. Others were [saying], "Look, I'll believe it when it happens." That kind of attitude made me want to do it even more. It acted as a kind of spur.'

Neil Franklin: 'People say to me, "You put business before life? You're crazy." But if I wanted to be a concert pianist I'd have to practise eight hours a day. It's no different in the business arena. People ask, "Don't you ever turn your phone off?" Business doesn't stop for me.'

Liz Meston: 'When you get knocked right back, you have to keep going and not be held back. You have to believe that's a hiccup and then go forward again. It's a "don't let the buggers get you down" sort of approach. From my friends, there was a lot of "Oh, she thinks she's a businesswoman" and there was a bit of a giggle behind my back when out came the briefcase. I tried not to listen.'

Nick Austin: 'I am the most impatient person in the world and as soon as I have achieved something I want to smash it up and do something better. It's a good trait in this industry and a personal characteristic that's allowed me to brand the culture – so that everyone understands that, unless we are creative and innovative and pushing ourselves to come up with the next best mousetrap, we won't be successful.'

Are entrepreneurs born, not made?

Nick Austin: 'All this gobbledegook about knowing you're an entrepreneur from the day you were born – I don't subscribe to that, but I think some people, through their environment, probably assume leadership roles more naturally.'

Neil Franklin: 'You can make a businessman; you can't make an entrepreneur. It's in you. With entrepreneurs, it's instinct. You have to be a lunatic – I mean that in the nicest possible way – because, if it was normal and ordinary, everyone would do it. The entrepreneur has a streak of madness that will take him to extremes. One moment he'll be studying, the next he'll be off setting up an airline. It's about going against the grain; when people say no you tend to say yes. None of my friends would take risks. They were saving money and earning fortunes compared with me, or doing nothing. I was between the two: I had no plans and no academic interest but I had an aptitude for learning. I'm like a sponge – I wanted to learn all the time. My concern about most business education is that there's too much time spent learning and not enough doing.'

ASSESS ONE

Quick list: In fewer than ten words, list

- your key personality traits
- your key skills
- previous enterprise experience
- why you want your own business
- what kind of business you want
- your key objectives in starting a business
- why you would be likely to succeed
- why you would be likely to fail as an entrepreneur

Quick list: List instances when you

- executed a decision promptly
- erred on the side of pessimism
- maintained enthusiasm despite disappointment
- coped with extreme pressure
- coped with extreme uncertainty
- worked long hours and still felt energised
- switched easily from tiny detail to 'big picture'
- spotted a solution that was not immediately apparent
- capitalised on an opportunity
- recognised your personal limitations
- calculated the risks involved in a venture
- made financial and other sacrifices
- were confident in presenting your ideas
- inspired people
- delegated responsibility

Chapter Two

How do entrepreneurs find and refine their ideas for business? Some businesses grow from passion; others from frustration. Where and how do people spot opportunities? Does an entrepreneur need experience in the industry he or she hopes to enter? Which business ideas will be successful? How can they be developed?

Do what you know

People who start successful businesses say that experience in the industry can help to minimise start-up risks. Sometimes an existing interest can be an efficient springboard into business, though it's important to consider the economics of a particular market and to realise that subject-related skills are not the same as business skills.

From an early age, **Richard Allen-Turner** enjoyed the humour of Spike Milligan and the Goons, and at school joined a band that played in a local pub. 'Instead of doing my homework, I'd be running around Worthing being chased by policemen – invaluable experience for later life.' At Thames Polytechnic he took his interest in comedy a stage further by organising student events, which led to a job on the union executive as entertainments officer booking new acts. From there it was a short step to joining **Jon Thoday**, representing performers.

> **20/20** . . . 'We tried to treat entertainment as a business when others treated it as a cosy cottage industry.'
>
> – Jon Thoday

Paul Varcoe and **Phil Docker** began to develop software for traders after spotting a gap in the market for a user-friendly system. When their workplace, LIFFE, changed its trading platform to go electronic, Docker, a broker, wanted to buy a new system but saw none that offered the functionality he wanted. 'No one had given much thought to the end user,' he explains. Meanwhile, Varcoe had developed his own handheld PC system to keep account of his trading options. 'Paul had developed this handheld system and I was pretty impressed, so I said, "Could we provide a better one?" Computer games were Paul's hobby and that's why our interface is so slick – he knows where the buttons should be.'

David Sproxton and **Peter Lord** developed a passion for animating while at school in Woking, making films in their spare time with a cine camera. 'As teenagers, we tried every camera technique under the sun,' recalls Sproxton. 'Pete was good at drawing, and I found light absolutely fascinating. In the summer vacation at university we carried on animating, just to earn some pin money.'

Martin Rutty and **Tim Gilbert** turned a spare-time passion into a full-time job after leaving school. 'At sixteen, we got into motorcycles and that cemented our friendship. We'd spend months taking motorcycles apart and putting them back together,' says Rutty. 'I went to university but it wasn't for me, so I left and went back to work as a courier.'

A year later, he started Speed Couriers, now known simply as Speed. Gilbert worked in the City before joining Rutty, and says, 'Martin woke me up to the idea that you could do anything. He said, "Come on, let's go and ride bikes" – and I saw it as a way of making a lot more money. He used to say, "I want to be a millionaire by the time I'm thirty." A lot of the time, I found myself thinking, "You can't do that" – but there was always Martin saying, "Watch me."'

The **Finn** twins drew on their passions for music and computers when as teenagers they began to develop their musical notation software. They realised there was a demand for their product and, after leaving university, tried to find someone to market it for them.

'Publishers were more interested in using it than selling it. Software companies said, "We don't know anything about music. Is there a market for this?" Offers came from people who saw the opportunity to make a fast buck, but we realised they didn't know enough about the technical side,' says **Jonathan Finn**. The pair decided to form their own company to produce the software.

Those already working in an industry often have a head start when developing a new business. **David Williams** was working for a power-generation company when he began to ponder renewable sources of energy. 'I went on to the board of a charity that looks after parrots, and spent time in the Dominican rainforest raising money for conservation. The clean air really struck me and made me realise that renewable sources of energy would bring together good business potential with environmental benefits.'

Robin Hutson was struck by the power of 'under expectation, over delivery' when he went for lunch in a pub near Primrose Hill, London. 'The pub was scruffy and the sofas were falling to bits, but we sat down and ordered goat's-cheese salad. That was several years ago but, at the time, to get a dish like that well executed in a pub was pretty much unheard of,' he says. 'The thing that was really obvious was for me to open a little country-house hotel but I knew it wasn't right and didn't fit. The mood was changing. All of a sudden, there was a different mode of eating, a more relaxed style combined with decent quality. I used to sit at home in the evenings quietly and try to think of an idea. Should I go to London? A townhouse? I started to think about bistros. And then we went to this gastro-pub, and it was very refreshing, and that really was a moment when I thought, "There's something in that." Shortly after, I was able to glue all these elements together – wine, bistro, townhouse, under expectancy.'

Trusting your taste

Roger Myers was working as an accountant as he began to think about opening his first bar. 'I think the restaurant entrepreneurs that are the greatest successes are those that do it subjectively,' he says. 'The restaurants which have done best and are most successful are those where the people who do them enjoy them. They're not doing them because they think someone else would do it that way. It's usually someone who has opened a bar they loved, their friends understood it and it appealed to them. And, because that person has been bright and operated it properly, they've survived.'

Brian Clivaz found his imagination sparked by Home House, a listed property north of Oxford Street that had been derelict for many years. At the time he was manager of the London restaurant Simpson's-in-the-Strand, and thinking of opening a private members' club. 'I was looking for somewhere to go. In the restaurant world you work funny hours and going out to eat wasn't much fun. I thought, "If I join a club, I can get away from all that." But the old clubs had waiting lists . . . modern places like the Groucho attracted a trendy media crowd and that didn't fit with me either. I decided to revisit the tired formula of gentlemen's clubs by ripping up the rule book and starting again – space, style and service being three key factors.'

> **20/20** . . . 'Business is not a science: it's definitely an art form. You can be successful in business by doing it by the rules, but that piece that creates the entity or idea out of nowhere – that's the wonderful part.'
> – Colin Halpern

Experiences of socialising in the capital also left **Terry Pullen** disenchanted. 'If you weren't in the in-crowd and were wearing the wrong clothes, you took the risk of being left outside in the rain.' Pullen already had a wine bar in south London, and a financial services company. 'I wanted to capitalise on my experience, take what I had locally into central London,' he explains. 'My clients from the City used to travel down to Beckenham for the evening and said if I put something like it on their doorstep, they'd back me.'

Jonathan Elvidge started The Gadget Shop out of a conviction that there was a gap in the market for a new kind of gift shop. 'I'd waited many years for somebody to open a shop like The Gadget Shop, because I would have a Christmas list for friends and family and wanted to get something they wouldn't expect – something fun. A real problem – and, talking to other people, I wasn't alone in this – was that men were difficult to buy presents for.' Another retail entrepreneur, **Mark Constantine**, started making his own cosmetics 'because I had a lack of trust in other people's'.

Jonathan Hartnell-Beavis and **James Millar** started their home-shopping business after noticing a dearth of food-delivery services in

London. 'My ideas usually come after a few pints. The idea for The Food Ferry came after a few *extra* pints,' says Hartnell-Beavis. 'I had people coming round to supper the next day and I hated going to the supermarket to buy things, particularly when I had a headache. In my frustration, I hunted through the *Yellow Pages* to find a company that would go to the shops for me, but I couldn't find anything.' Millar adds, 'Food shopping was a nightmare, even for a couple of bachelors buying two Fray Bentos and a packet of chips. Nobody would help you when they changed the displays. There were always queues. We thought, "There are days of unoccupied time here." '

> **20/20** . . . 'A little knowledge is a dangerous thing and sometimes with a good idea you need to plough on regardless. If you are made aware of some of the difficulties or potential pitfalls, you might not have the energy or enthusiasm to overcome them.'
>
> – Philip Newton

Moving the market on

An ideal market is probably already large or ready to grow. **Colin Halpern** describes two scenarios.

'One is a very established market, where very often there's minimal or no growth and you are going to be taking business from other people. The other is where you see the market today is £15 million but it looks like this market in five years is going to be £200 million. Now you have a whole different set of dynamics, which makes it far more exciting but also far more difficult to survive in, because things move so fast.'

Liz Meston says she and **Juliana Galvin** were lucky to hit upon a market with few direct competitors. Other entrepreneurs choose markets supplied by inefficient or out-of-date products. While training to be a social worker, **Charlotte Barker** saw the need to refresh the educational-games market. 'One college assignment I had was to look at working with resources which are currently around you. I realised that community groups had board games that they were using with young people, but there wasn't really anything that grabbed my attention – they were standard and pretty boring. I bought myself some cardboard and paints, and made my own game. Over the years I became aware of what the gap in the market was – because I knew that the resources that people were using were exactly the same ones that they had always used previously.'

Will King suffered from razor burn and became frustrated that shaving products had not moved with the times. 'I was working in advertising and I had to wear a white shirt. I was always getting blood on it, so my wife, Ann, suggested that I put some oil under my shaving gel, because it was a good lubricant. That was when I started to think about developing a new product – shaving products hadn't really advanced in twenty years.'

Do business ideas need to be original? Not at all, says **Marshall King**. 'Our business was creating a new e-market in construction, so inventing something that made money was the greatest problem. We had to provide a stable business growth plan so that IT developers could develop against it and so requirements weren't changing every two months, and find good people with the right experience as well as convincing customers that we had a solution for their problem. My advice would be to do something that you know works, because there are other companies doing it already. It's far easier to be a bit better than other people than to invent a new business. By doing something that you know works, you eliminate one of the largest risks.'

20/20 . . . 'A great thing is to never be afraid to use other people's ideas.'

– Barry Bester

David Landau modelled *Loot* on a newspaper that he saw at Milan airport in 1984. 'I got to London, took a taxi and stopped off at every newsagent on the way home. Nobody had ever heard of a free-ads paper,' he recalls. The restaurateur **Roger Myers** went to America often and says he would always come back with plenty of ideas. 'Everybody's a plagiarist. You think, "I'll try this idea and that idea" . . . Café Rouge started as the son of Dôme, incorporating all the good bits that we thought we could repeat.'

Developing an idea

What differentiates a business concept that sounds good from one that actually works and will make money? **Juliana Galvin** and **Liz**

Meston considered many ideas for business, ranging from selling quails' eggs to spinning fabric. But in 1990 they had a more pressing problem: both wanted to offload second-hand curtains, but they couldn't find a seller – so they started up The Curtain Exchange.

Richard Reed brainstormed several ideas with his friends before they came up with a real need. 'On holiday, we were all feeling knackered and someone said, "When was the last time we ate anything good?" We began thinking about making fruit drinks.'

> **20/20** . . . 'I have always been clear that something was going to work for me, somewhere, and I have tried many different things.'
>
> – John Mortimer

Peter Lammer and **Jan Hruska** met as postdoctoral students at Oxford and spent months developing a laptop computer in the eighties, but eventually shelved the project. They turned to software, and to encryption. Even that took a while to get off the ground, says Lammer. 'We thought we could write a product and everyone would want it, which now seems completely naïve. We went through some pretty soul-searching days when it wasn't clear that the software business was going to take off . . . We thought about going into a completely different area of business, and looked at importing crockery from Italy or trading coal and soda ash with the Russians and the Chinese. Fortunately, we didn't get sidetracked, but there were certainly times when the software business looked unpromising.'

> **20/20** . . . 'What's needed is the ability to link an idea, a concept or a belief with discipline and to an actual business plan. That is the true difference between a good idea and a business that makes money.'
>
> – Terry Pullen

Dan Morrell hung on to an idea that took six years to come to fruition. He was in his early twenties, and recuperating from a serious car accident, when he came up with the idea of planting trees, based on a theory that trees can help to offset carbon dioxide emissions. He wanted individuals and corporations to pay for the plantings and take responsibility for pollution. He started by taking the plan to motoring organisations. One organisation bought the idea but did nothing with it. Three years later, Morrell bought it back and tried to raise interest in other quarters, before starting his own venture, Future Forests. 'In the early days,' he reflects, 'the easiest thing would have been to have another idea and give up on the one I had.'

Carol Dukes wrote a business plan for a gardening venture in 1996, but then began thinking about how to apply the model to other markets. 'I was working in the Internet space and spending a lot of time thinking about new business ideas, and it occurred to me that the shape of business that could really work well on the Internet was one where the purchase required a lot of information that you couldn't easily provide in a bricks-and-mortar environment, but electronically it would work well. The best situation is where there's a greater range of products than you can economically stock in one location.

'Gardening happened to fit that model but I said in the business plan that it would apply equally well to other sectors such as alternative health.'

With the new availability of venture capital in the late nineties, she started up ThinkNatural. 'I had spent time thinking about how difficult it is to do the fulfilment of plants, because the complexities made it less attractive, whereas alternative health – a box of pills – was relatively simple,' she explains.

It's not easy to know which ideas will develop into successful products or drive a business forward, says **Colin Halpern**. 'What may be a good thought six months ago is not a good thought six months later, but there's often no true way of determining whether your thought or idea is worthwhile. The big organisations spend fortunes on trying to determine whether they should build something – and history says to them, "You're a bunch of turkeys." The most fundamental aspect is that there's got to be gross profit. You've got to sell something for more than you pay for it.'

Asked to define what distinguishes a good business idea from a bad one, **Jon Moulton** remarks that 'a large available market is about the only consistent thing. I have seen people make successes out of terrible concepts and other people screw up perfectly good concepts.'

Andy Hobsbawm notes, 'Something my dad once told me: you don't create by waiting to be inspired. Similarly, opportunity never happens when you sit around and wait for it: it waits for you to commit to other plans. I also believe in the power of quality. Truly great ideas have a magic and energy all their own – an inspirational and creative force that everybody is drawn to. On the other hand, there's an old truism that a good idea well executed will always beat a great idea poorly implemented. Often it's better to just get on and do something than fuss and fiddle until it's just right. Perfectionism can definitely slow you down and the process of evolution and improving something along the way can be just as interesting as the final result.'

Terry Pullen says it's important to give yourself space to develop ideas. 'Take the idea, test it and don't be afraid to change it. There's no way in the world that some of the best working models, at the moment when they were conceived as purely an idea, were ever in the same shape as they are now. You've got to start with something. If you get into the mindset of rejecting ideas, you cripple your natural abilities as an entrepreneur. You shouldn't ever inhibit this process, because ideas improve things, motivate people and make you the company to work for, as against your competitors.'

> **20/20** . . . 'I originally came to London with £50 in my pocket thinking 'I'll just work it out'. If you ever think too hard about something, you probably wouldn't do it.'
>
> – William Sargent

Kevin Bulmer says the common denominator 'is that a good idea really drives itself'.

For some people, the problem lies in choosing which brilliant idea to go with. **Sue Welland** observes, 'The difference between a good idea and a business idea is that you can work out how to make money out of it. You can see that there could be an audience and where the suppliers are, and begin to see how to make money.'

An entrepreneur may have a fantastic idea, but taking the final steps to set up a business can be like peering over a cliff. Knowing the dangers of the market, **Nick Austin** and **Alan Bennie** agonised over the decision. 'It's like cutting the umbilical cord – since the age of twenty-one I had been in a job and had an income,' says Austin. 'It's hard to make the jump. When you're working in a business it's a very social thing: you go in and you're working with a team of people and it's fun that way. Suddenly, as an entrepreneur, you're sitting at your kitchen table and you push aside your bowl of cornflakes and you sit there and think, "Right, what do I do now? This is Day One of the rest of my life."

'It's a pretty lonely existence at first. That's why it's really important to have a sense of belief in what you are doing – you will need it because there will be moments of hell.'

For **Jonathan Elvidge** there came a point where there was no choice but to leave his job and press forward with his idea. 'I thought I'd hire people to run the first Gadget Shop. That never happened because a photo was printed in the local paper which showed me in a hard hat, holding a model of the shop, captioned, THE FIRST LOCAL RETAILER. My employers hadn't known about my plans, and I was asked to speak to the managing director. I was told that I couldn't do both [jobs], so I left. It's the same with anyone who progresses hard towards the fulfilment of a dream, goal or idea – you just do what's right for that, without a lot of thought for the consequences.'

QUESTIONS FROM THE EDGE

Do you have to be passionate about your business idea?

Daniel Gestetner: 'In a start-up business you have got to be excited about the product – you have to put in twenty-four hours, seven days a week.'

Sue Welland: 'When you're in a brand-new market, you need to be interested in and excited by the idea because it's going to absorb two hundred per cent of you – if you were only motivated by money, there's other ways of making it.'

Carol Dukes: 'I think the idea has ideally got to be something that you like. But this idea that you've got to fall in love with your product – this idea of "I love it, everyone else will love it, so it will work" – is wrong. A lot of start-ups fall over, whether they're restaurants or wine-importing businesses, because people don't look at the economics.'

James Millar: 'It's most likely to be successful if it really comes from the heart. If something seems quite a good idea but you wouldn't necessarily do it yourself, then you are simply an employee or an adviser because when the chips are down it's so much easier to jack it all in or throw your hands up and say to someone else, "It was your idea." Flip it the other way and assume that you are a customer. Would you be interested in the idea if it came to you in some format? The answer must be reasonably clear. That was really the direction that we came from – we were hacked-off customers and we thought, "There must be an alternative." '

Martin Rutty: 'Choose something you like doing and then work out how you can make money at it. Don't do it the other way around. I could be a dentist or a chiropodist if I had the qualifications, but I wouldn't make a penny because I would loathe going to work. Make sure that you position yourself in an industry that you can make some money in.'

How much experience do I need in the market I want to enter?

Roger Myers: 'In the restaurant industry I don't think it's true that you need experience yourself, and I wouldn't discourage anyone from going into it just because they have no experience. I was an accountant in the music business previously, and my partner and myself opened a bar because it was something we liked. We made all the usual mistakes but we did bring in someone that did know about running bars.'

Charlie Muirhead: 'Going into the tech market as the founder of a company, you had better be pretty comfortable about being able to interpret the needs of your customers and mapping those needs or requirements to the technology in the marketplace. Later in the company that's important, but, early on, that's absolutely crucial.'

John Mortimer: 'It depends entirely on the circumstances and what you do with them. Even if you haven't got experience, you need to ensure that you're clear about what you're going to do. However, the main thing is to get on and do it, rather than not do it.'

Should I act immediately to implement an idea?

Richard Reed: 'As soon as I have an idea, I will not act on it for a day. A lot of the time, ideas that immediately seem brilliant are not clearly of intrinsic value. Overnight, your brain calms down and you're not so excited. If the idea sticks and seems like a good idea the next day, it probably is. And if you have good elements within your idea, make sure you stick to it and don't let anyone water it down.'

Is there a right time to launch my idea?

Andy Hobsbawm: 'Follow your instincts and your passions. If you really believe that something needs doing in the world and you are passionate about doing it, then you're far more likely to be successful. Don't worry too much about 'the right time for a business opportunity'. Nobody has a clue, really. All financial experts can tell you is that markets will go up, down or stay the same!'

David Landau: 'I think if an idea is as good as *Loot* was, it can happen at any time. The market is always ripe for ideas that are independent of fashion and short-term prospects. If you have invented the wheel, it doesn't matter if you launch it in March or September. If it's a particular type of air-conditioning, that's different.'

ASSESS TWO

- Think of ideas relating to an area you know through an existing interest; consider adapting professional skills
- Brainstorm with friends; don't dismiss simple ideas
- Look for inspiration at home and abroad
- It's easier to better what's already been done – particularly when a market is dominated by old-fashioned or inefficient solutions
- Look for a growing or large market: Are there leading brands? How loyal are customers to brands?

- How will your product stand out? What will customers be prepared to pay?
- Guard a good idea, but if necessary amend your model or apply it to a different market

Quick list: Take your shortlist of ideas and describe for each

- how it will work
- what it will look like
- how much it might cost to produce
- how much you might be able to sell it for
- how many units you can sell and how fast
- the current state of the market
- the experience you have in that market

Chapter Three

This chapter looks at how people form partnerships for business. Those with previous start-up experience may opt to go solo but others prefer to share responsibilities and risks. Who do people choose to go into business with? What qualities do they look for? What makes a successful partnership tick?

Lone traders

Shawn Taylor had a clear vision from a young age. He spent ten years on the racing circuit and started his business at the age of 28. Severe dyslexia meant he left school with no qualifications.

'I was saving up from thirteen to race bikes. I didn't come from a rich background, and it was a big family, so I took various jobs to raise money to race. Once I've got something in my head, I carry it all the way through.'

He was offered places in teams but realised he would have to raise more money to compete at higher levels. 'The important thing was to keep racing but it got to a stage where the only way I could get further was to fund it myself. My work was unskilled, so I sat down and thought, "I've got to get something sorted."' He went to college for two years, then wrote a business plan and set up his first vehicle service centre, with the eventual aim of setting up his own race team as part of the business.

'I was told, from a legal point of view, to avoid partners. If someone isn't pulling their weight, it's a risk,' he says. 'A lot of people haven't actually got it in them to get their own business because it's a very unsafe environment: you never know what's round the corner and you're putting everything on the line. This was my idea and I didn't want anyone coming in with a lot of money and stealing that. I've sacrificed a lot in my life and, once it takes off, I want to be there to get the rewards.

'As a sole trader, you have to be stubborn. You have to know what you want and unfortunately you have to open yourself up for a lot of worry, so you have to be mentally strong as well.'

James Keay says he would never go as far as fifty–fifty with another partner. 'Probably it's control: I like to be able to make the decisions. It's not that I am greedy but what I have done has worked. You need key managers but having a partner is not really necessary. Maybe I've just been lucky but I've never felt the need and I didn't want to feel reliant on anyone. Everything I've done has been on my own – I just get on and do it.'

Neil Franklin, who has worked with partners and without them, points out, 'As an entrepreneur, it's a lonely road and you need support, but actually you don't need a partner. When you're young it's always easier to share with one, but you only know you don't want a partner when you've already had one. The problem with partners is that you expect them to be the same as you, which is lunacy. You only have to look at personal relationships to see that you have to try a few times before you get it right.

'The guys I was in business with previously had the same qualities and the same interests, but I was dealing with twenty years of their history and twenty years of my history. You end up in a position where you put so much faith in the business relationship that the expectations spiral out of proportion; then you split up. Two people can drive a business further than one but partnerships only work when you're fully attuned with each other, when you have the same goals, drive, ambition and, most importantly, commitment. Business partners can be closer than marital partners because you spend all day with each other, and often all weekend socialising.'

20/20 . . . 'To be a lone entrepreneur, you need a huge amount of self-belief and, correspondingly, a great lack of self-doubt.'
– Carol Dukes

Old friends, new alliances

Some partnerships form at an early age and continue into adulthood. As children, brothers **Ben** and **Jonathan Finn** collaborated to develop various ideas from 'rockets that never quite left the ground' to an electric burglar alarm and software versions of board games, and went on to develop and sell their music software Sibelius.

The partners behind the drinks company Innocent met at university, and business formed a key strand in their friendship. **Richard Reed** describes how, when they left to take corporate jobs, 'every weekend, we would talk about how great it would be to have our own business'. **Mark Jackson** and **Michael Symons** played squash together, but business came into the partnership only later on. 'Michael and I were friends before we started the company. We had fun in each other's company and we found each other to be intellectually challenging,' says Jackson.

While for some a business partnership evolves from friendship, other people seek a partner for a specific reason, such as expertise or finance. **John Frieda** recalls that he 'didn't have a clue about marketing and distribution' and told his future partner, **Gail Federici**, 'I don't want to reinvent the wheel and make mistakes that don't need to be made. I'd rather have a partner who's already gone through this.'

Hugh Agnew and **Charles Marshall** met as students in the early seventies, and twenty years later Agnew asked Marshall for assistance. They soon became business partners. 'It was a very difficult time for me,' says Agnew. 'I'd parted with my partners and took the opportunity to buy out our Yeoman technology. I needed to raise £150,000 in six weeks. Charles was one of three or four people I rang. We spent a day looking at this business plan and he said, "Look, I think this could be done." '

Marshall had just returned from Japan with the aim of becoming an investor. 'A week after I left Bankers Trust, Hugh called me. We weren't the kind of buddies who would speak every week, and he didn't know I'd left my job, so his timing was impeccable. He gave me a brief outline of what he planned to do. I thought it sounded interesting and said I would help.'

If partners have worked as a team already, risks of starting up can lessen. **Keith Hobbs** and **Linzi Coppick** started their design firm in

1994 but loyalty developed several years earlier, says Hobbs. 'When I first met Linzi and offered her a job, I asked whether she wanted to start on the first day of the next month. A week later, I found myself very busy and thought, "I could do with Linzi." I phoned her and said, "I wonder if you could start earlier than I suggested." She gave me a reply very significant in forming our relationship: "Give me an hour." My relationship with Linzi grew most solidly when we were on the other side of the fence, out on our own. We had a good business relationship and the vision grew out of that friendship.'

When **William Carey** was offered the chance to set up a unit trust company, he asked his colleague **Nigel Legge** to join him. 'We decided together that this was something we would like to do,' says Carey. Legge says the pair created 'an environment where you could respect and work with each other's strengths and weaknesses. That's why William and I have stuck together for so long.'

Colleagues **Nicola Murphy** and **Jane Wynn** left their jobs to set up River Publishing with two other partners, who ran another business. 'For the first couple of years Jane and I got on relatively well with our other two partners,' says Murphy. 'It started to be a less easy partnership after four years and by five, it was uncomfortable. At that point we bought them out. One partner was a close friend of mine, which is one of the reasons we went into business with him, and because of what happened we lost that friendship. Conversely, Jane and myself weren't close friends at all. From our experience I would say, "Don't go into business with friends, but go into business with people you respect for other reasons." '

Sometimes partnerships are forged through pressure rather than friendship. **Will King** and **Herbie Dayal** teamed up after Dayal, a management consultant, made King redundant from his job. 'Herbie recommended closing the company I was working for,' says King. 'When I left, he said, "Keep in touch." I liked him – he came across as genuine.'

Dayal was impressed by King's ability to face realities. 'Will phoned and asked me straight, "What does the situation look like?" I told him it didn't look good. Often, in that event, people will keep their heads down, but Will wanted to know what was going on.' Later, Dayal decided to back King's new venture. 'He came back to me with his shaving oil in a little bottle and told me, "This really works." He was dead certain and wanted to get on with it.'

Jonathan Elvidge formed a partnership with **Andrew Hobbs**, the man from whom he rented his first retail unit. 'Andy seemed a powerful figure. He was the guy who spelled success or failure,' remembers Elvidge. Hobbs says Elvidge 'behaved like a retailer even though he didn't have a shop. I'd ask some people who were running retail operations, "What's your turnover last week in Barnstaple?" and they wouldn't have a clue. I'd say, "What's your margin?" "I don't know." Jon had a scrapbook where he had cut out from magazines things he wanted to sell. I would say, "How much do these cost?" and he'd say, "It's £5 and I think I can sell it for £10." '

> **20/20** . . . 'I would rather have fifty per cent of something that could be very big than a hundred per cent of something that might never have got beyond one store.'
>
> – Jonathan Elvidge

Shared enthusiasm can also spark a partnership. **Liz Meston** recalls that, every time she met **Juliana Galvin**, 'the one thing that really buzzed was that we were always trying to start our own little businesses. The first time we met, at a lunch party, we talked business with another girl. By the end of that discussion, the girl was flat out on the sofa, bored stiff, but we were still talking.'

Andrew Gerrie approached **Mark Constantine** in the late eighties to ask if he could take the Cosmetics to Go (CTG) concept to Australia. 'He had a twinkle in his eye; he kept phoning up and saying did I want to do something?' says Constantine. The pair eventually became partners in Lush. 'The group that had been involved in CTG was drifting back together and putting out some ideas, but they only wanted to do stuff on a fairly small basis,' says Gerrie. 'I told them I'd come and have a look. I liked Mark – he had presence and experience, and he was very opinionated. There wasn't all this dancing around like you get in a lot of relationships. It wasn't "Let's do lunch": it was "Let's do business".'

Second time around

When **Julian Richer** met **Alan McGee** at a dinner party, both were successful entrepreneurs. 'I had read that Alan was leaving Creation Records and going freelance, and I couldn't believe this guy was coming to dinner,' recalls Richer. 'The chance of meeting someone when the time is right is quite small. I'd been keen for a while to get into other businesses but what made me excited was that someone of Alan's calibre was available.' The pair subsequently launched the Poptones record label. 'I would never have got involved in the record business without someone good as a partner – I'm old enough to know that you can only do one big thing in life yourself,' says Richer. 'Meeting Alan when he'd just left Creation – you don't get a better opportunity than that.'

Richard Seymour and **Dick Powell** met as lecturers at art college and eventually shared an office, but at first they were reluctant to form a partnership. 'Dick came back from a holiday one year to find me [in his office],' says Seymour. 'That was the crucible where Seymour Powell was formed. He came in one morning and said, "Look, I've got an idea. I think we should form a company together. I think we should call it Seymour Powell." I thought, "Here's how to win a man over, with my name at the beginning."'

Powell continues, 'We were working together on projects but, because both of us had been burned in previous businesses, we didn't want to have partners ever again. After three years of gradually growing together, we formalised the arrangement. We were working together in the best way that partners can. It was by osmosis: his thinking was penetrating mine, and vice versa.'

20/20 . . . 'If you get people working together who have been independent for quite a long time, the thing that cracks a partnership most quickly is when you step heavily on each other's toes. If you have a partnership with somebody who has a tendency to be equally unorthodox, you have to trust that person enough to say, "That's your bit."'

– Hugh Osmond

Robert Eitel had already launched and built one successful fashion label when he met **Anne Storey**. 'I was looking to start another label, or to license some American labels,' says Eitel, 'and I met with Anne's tutor at the Royal College of Art and said, "This is the sort of person I'm looking for. Have you any ideas?" I wanted someone with experience and she pointed me in Anne's direction.' Storey was about to leave Nicole Farhi and agreed to meet Eitel. 'I went to see him with an open mind. The idea evolved gradually, not immediately. I liked it that Robert wasn't just a flash in the pan. A few months would go by, and then he would ring. I think he saw me as someone settled, someone who would be prepared to get involved in a long-term project. During that time, we talked about how we might start a collection. After fifteen months, the label got going. It wasn't an overnight decision: it was very much thought-out.'

Roles

While partners must share a vision for business, identical skills and temperaments are not necessarily advantageous. **Dan Morrell** recalls, 'With Sue [Welland], I felt my project had a much better chance of happening because she would get it under control. I will go off on a creative rant and she is a balancer.'

Welland adds, 'When somebody sets me up with an idea, I pull it together and network to make it happen. I'll never let something drop until I've flogged it to death. Dan has a hundred ideas a day. Ninety-nine will be nonstarters, but he won't know which is which – that's where I come in. With partners, you've got to be clear about who's managing what and who's responsible for what so that you're not relying on your friendship instinct to grow the company. I managed the marketing and public relations messages and he was the showman. I like to be the number two – that's where I always wanted to be, providing all the planning, and Dan can then go out and present it.'

Richard Reed says he and his two partners had aptitude and experience in different business disciplines. 'There's no point in all doing the same task. Fortunately, none of us want to do the other's job, although we never consciously decided those roles. We can also afford to be painfully honest with each other. We have the biggest arguments because we are such good friends and we don't hold back. We have only come to blows over the colour of the floor in the office; we have never debated the principles upon which we run.'

Will King and **Herbie Dayal** made a point of learning by doing. 'With Herbie's training as an accountant, you would have expected him to run our payments system, but I've been doing that for years,' says King. 'He made me do the business plan in the early days to find out how much money I was going to lose.'

The idea was to learn, says Dayal. 'At first, when you set up, you think there's a whole world of experts who know exactly what they're doing, but at the end of the day you realise you can do it. If you don't understand your own business plan, you won't really understand your business. Will decides on all the payments, though it's not what he would naturally think of doing. Sales and presentation would normally be Will's bag, but he was keen that I do more of that side. I'm not a product designer, or anything like that, but it's to do with having a vision and saying, "This is how I think it ought to be." '

Differences in temperament and style can become sources of strength for a business. **James Sommerville** explains, 'Simon [Needham] can make a decision in ten seconds. I would rather read a couple of pages of A4 and maybe even sleep on it. Sometimes we need his approach and to be swift, sometimes mine – when we can't shoot from the hip. Respect comes from knowing that we meet in the middle.'

James Millar provides another illustration. 'I'm naturally more of an adviser. I like to tease out a problem. Jonathan [Hartnell-Beavis] is utterly the other way around. He's a complete doer. My vision is of him getting his hands dirty, completely stuck in, something I completely disagree with. Answering the phone every twenty seconds is not something I want to spend my life doing, but Jonathan loves doing it. He wants to find out what the problem is and find practical solutions. I would far rather say, "If we're getting twenty-five calls, we've got a general problem that we need to address."

'We each operate on an entirely different basis. Neither is wrong, so long as you can accept that there are different ways of working with the same net result. I would go further and say we have a pretty good combination because of that. If we both jumped into the warehouse at every given opportunity or always dived for the telephone, we wouldn't have any future strategy. If we were always planning, we wouldn't get anything done.'

Robin Hutson and **Gerard Basset** say their success is built on continuous communication. 'If there's one thing we have done right, it's to talk. It is like a marriage – if you keep talking, you're unlikely to misunderstand each other,' says Hutson. 'Gerard has always been brilliant at saying, "We haven't had a chat for a while. Let's have a glass of wine together." We talk about everything and we know how the other is thinking. We don't live in each other's pockets but

Gerard will ring me and say, "When have you got an hour to sit down and talk?" About a week after we opened in Winchester, he said, "We're trying to do too much business here. We're trying to please everyone. We should take it easier."

'That's a brave thing to say after a week, because your natural instinct is, "Let's get them in and the money in the till." Gerard taught me there's always another side to the story. My instinct would have been to fill the restaurant up, but he suggested we took things steadily, did it properly and made sure the people who did come through had a good experience. He was absolutely right, and hence we have a loyal following of customers.'

Often entrepreneurs talk about the importance of pitching their ideas to each other. 'An employee would probably agree with whatever I said, but Andy [Hobbs] as a partner will really question things,' says **Jonathan Elvidge**. 'The times I've been nervous about taking the next step, having Andy there to combine thoughts with has been a great strength. If either of us has an idea we want to carry forward, we'll sell it to each other.'

Space and pace

Problems may arise in a partnership when one doesn't work as hard or thinks another is not as capable. Some problems simply grow from overfamiliarity. After seven years together, **William Sieghart** and **Neil Mendoza** called in a psychologist when their relationship began to sour. 'We had what I can only describe as an itch. We found ourselves getting on each other's nerves,' says Sieghart. 'We began to be at our happiest when the other one was away, which meant that you had the whole toy box to yourself,' adds Mendoza. 'Lots of tension would build up if the other person was in the room.

'We are both incredibly competitive. We even used to argue about who was the most competitive. That's when we got the shrink in, the equivalent of a life coach, who laid us down on sofas and we resolved it in about five minutes. It was literally talking about the problem with a third person that solved it and we've done that kind of thing again since. After seven years we just got a bit bored of each other. If you work next to each other for a long time, partners often fall out. Spice Girls break up. There's going to be tension.'

Not all competitiveness is destructive. **Richard Seymour** describes a healthier kind of pressure, 'a sort of relay . . . we always have to come up with one better'.

> **20/20** . . . 'We actively disagree about lots of things and we have long debates to work them out, but, if you win, you win; if you lose, you just get on with it.'
>
> – Mark Jackson

Barry Bester and **Stuart Williams** are separated by an age gap of thirteen years and this, says Bester, means 'we don't compete to see who's king of the pile'. 'It's an important and beneficial thing,' says Williams, 'because we avoid the father–son conflicts and sibling rivalry which you might otherwise get. We are able to relate to each other's experiences but I am also able to pass on knowledge that I've accumulated without build-up of resentment.'

The founders of ATTIK spent a year apart during a period of growth, opening studios in different continents. 'It was hard for a patch when Simon and I were never in the same town,' says **James Sommerville**. 'As the business grew, Simon moved to London, I moved to New York, then he moved to Sydney. He was asleep when I was awake, and vice versa, and we weren't concentrating on the growth of the business. All we were doing was firefighting in respective offices.' There wasn't much communication during that time, says **Simon Needham**. 'That meant a lot of things didn't get done, because we weren't debating and planning. We realised we had to rectify that.'

The pair eventually agreed to give up their roles as individual managing directors and develop roles as group leaders. 'We have come full circle now,' says Sommerville. 'We spend more time together now than in the last ten years. Even if you have to jump in a plane just to go and hang out for a couple of days, you need to do that. If nothing else, you're sharing things that are problems or opportunities and bouncing things around. If you do that every three or four months . . . you are on the same level, sharing ideas.'

> **20/20** . . . 'We've sat in the same room for [more than] seven years and have become very close, as you do when you listen to each other's telephone conversations.'
>
> – Jonathan Kennedy

Mark Constantine says he found it 'horrendous' when **Andrew Gerrie** went to Australia for eighteen months to build their Asia-Pacific operations: 'All the business things he did out there were superb and he helped get the Japanese business off to a flying start, but that eighteen months seemed like forever. I was nervous the whole time. If I got up early, he was all ready to go to bed and, from us talking three times a day, it went down to hardly any communication.

'Having a partner is like having a comfort blanket. You can work out what to do on your own but it's sharing the decision making that counts.' Before he went, Gerrie said he believed that the move would be 'tough, but good for the growth of the business'. Constantine says the separation was also good for the partnership – Gerrie eventually came back to the UK. 'I tend to take more direction from Andrew than I did before and I try to support him more than before. We probably argue less and, when we do have heated discussions, we usually end up seeing eye to eye, and I see what's winding him up.'

Andrew Pollock talks of the benefits of distance in a new partnership. 'In the beginning Simon [Rees] and I didn't know each other socially, and we didn't rush into that kind of relationship. Once we knew our partnership was going to work, we got more friendly.' **Brett Gosper** is aware of the need to prevent burn-out as time passes. 'Mark [Wnek] and I used to see a lot more of each other outside work but, as much as we like seeing each other a lot, we don't want to get on each other's nerves.'

Others, like **David Rhodes** and **Chris Snowden**, opt to keep business and personal lives entirely distinct. 'David is a very private person,' says Snowden. 'I can remember going out for a drink in the pub with him in 1975 but by 1978 he wasn't doing that any more. It was the right thing to do. If you don't hedge your private life, you find it disappears into the work. I've tended to separate the two as well.'

Trevor Horn and **Jill Sinclair** married and went into business together a year or so later. 'When my partner left me, I said to Jill, "The good thing is that you can manage me now," ' recalls Horn. 'Fifteen seconds after I appointed her, she told me I would have to give up trying to be an artist and concentrate on being a producer. One reason she and I work well together is that we leave each other alone. Jill runs the business and I make records, though we are always discussing. Being with her is almost like being on my own.'

Kate Copestake and Kevin Bulmer, both business and domestic partners, have their own way of dealing with the intrusion of their business into their weekend lives: they have talked of how, each Sunday afternoon, they climb into their double Jacuzzi at home, open a bottle of champagne and spend several hours discussing their business. 'It's where we polish over any cracks,' says Copestake. 'People ask, "How do you live, work and play together?" I couldn't imagine any other way.'

What happens when you find yourself working not just with your partner, but the whole family? 'The way we square the circle as a family is to have a financial democracy,' says Jack Morris, whose four brothers are all involved in the same business. 'We're all equal shareholders and we all earn exactly the same salary, irrespective of seniority or contribution. All we ask is that we each give our all in the area designated to work in. It puts a great peer pressure on each brother if someone's not pulling their weight – that doesn't happen often but it gingers them up.

'Running a business on your own is a lonely game unless you can share the pleasure with people close to you. I love the opportunity, as I have all the time, of sitting down with my four brothers and talking through problems as a co-operative. Occasionally a brother has expressed interest in doing something else and breaking out of the business. We'll say, "That's fine, but don't expect us to be quite so interested if you're doing it for yourself." When it comes down to it, they realise that severing the family relationship is too high a price to pay for personal gain. The group is big enough for all of us to make our mark without tripping over each other.'

It isn't always so smooth. For Karen Haddon, 'having had an outsider in the boardroom, I've seen the family problem more clearly. When you're family, you cross lines of familiarity that you don't cross otherwise. When it gets personal you take it home and, under those circumstances, your relationships change. It was unnatural for me to challenge my father [in the boardroom] and it's definitely changed our relationship. Out of choice, I wouldn't do it again. My daughter said to me, "I want to join the business," and I said, "You'll do it without me."'

QUESTIONS FROM THE EDGE

What do you look for in a partner, and why look for one?

Terry Pullen: 'The first thing to identify is the skill sets that complement your own. You also need to identify whether that person shares your belief and whether it's someone that you can intrinsically get on with. My own requirement in a partner is very simple: money. I think any entrepreneur is a liar if he doesn't admit that he wants a hundred per cent of something if he can get it. The true entrepreneur wants control because that's a major part of his personality. He may then want to incentivise key people to have ownership.'

Sue Welland: 'I like the sense of "you're in it together". When you're pushing a rock up a hill, it's nice to do it with someone and for them to understand exactly how you feel.'

Mark Constantine: 'I don't think there are any rules for finding a partner – only to look at your psychological profiles but, even then, Andrew [Gerrie] and I don't match the criteria. I always think there's a strong need in most entrepreneurs to create a large family. It often replaces family that they don't have, which for me is true but not for Andrew.'

Should you team up with friends to start a company?

Richard Reed: 'You have to differentiate between a mate and a really close friend. Before becoming partners, we had been close friends at college and knew each other's faults and characters.'

Carol Dukes: 'The finance director who was with us for the first year and a half is a great personal friend. I found it great to have her around, but also had respect for her professionally. It's harder if you go into business with a chum and find they are not up to the job.'

Liz Meston: 'Juliana [Galvin] and I weren't friends but we knew each other and that was the best way, because you sometimes know your friends too well. We became friends through the business. It's fun when we see each other socially but that's not often. It's important that we keep separate identities.'

Andrew Pollock: 'If you start off as friends, it's more fraught with danger. Simon [Rees] and I started as colleagues and developed into friends. We had the luxury of being able to do that. If you start from a friendship point of view, I would advise people to take great care. From time to time, you have to have some serious discussions about how the business is going to go – and you do need to have those.'

ASSESS THREE

- In starting up a business you can choose to be a sole trader, partnership, limited company or collective
- In seeking a partner, look for someone who can balance your own skills and temperament
- With your business partner, draw up a written agreement with a solicitor to cover issues such as profits, tasks, tax matters and new partners
- Don't rush into a partnership – trust your instincts

Quick list: Do you need a partner?

- Do you worry about protecting your idea and profits?
- To you, would a partner minimise risk or be a liability?
- Have you skills and experience in sufficient areas to be successful alone?
- Do you tend to seek reassurance when things are tough?
- Would you rather have employees than equals?
- Do you have support from a domestic partner or family?
- Will you grow the business at a fast enough rate by yourself?

Quick list: Have you found the ideal partner?

- Do you talk easily and frequently?
- Can you argue without fighting?

- Is it clear who will manage which areas?
- Are you competitive? If so, is it healthy?
- Can you work effectively apart?
- Do you respect each other?
- Do you enjoy each other's company?
- Are your levels of commitment similar?
- Are you equally flexible?
- Do you have complementary working styles?
- Can you give each other sufficient space?

PART TWO

PREPARING FOR TAKE-OFF

Chapter Four

The next step is to take a business idea from a scribble on the back of an envelope, through to research and planning. Who will offer the best advice? How much work should go into the business plan? Who will be the customers of the business?

Researching the market

Anyone starting a business needs to demonstrate an understanding of the market, and the place of their product within it. For **Carol Dukes**, who started up a mail-order business supplying natural health products, it was nearly impossible to get data.

'Our market is very hard to research. You have to pull bits and pieces from here and there, and it would be hard to research even if we had a full-scale team. Our customer base was not necessarily one that pre-existed.

'We reforecast monthly – we have to – but, when you start something that doesn't exist, you have no data by definition . . . you have to make do with common sense. You say, "Let's assume this" or "Let's assume that" and "What if it doesn't happen this way?" Then you have to just get going. It's almost impossible for the reality to match the plan exactly. It's not like running a gold mine or a shipping company, where planning and forecasting is an exact science. It doesn't matter how long you take over planning, because it's not knowledge that you can go and find. It's all about managing uncertainty.'

One of the first ways to get a feel for a market is to evaluate the competition. When **Roger Myers** began opening Café Rouge outlets, he did his research by dining out with his wife. 'We used to see whether a site was near a PizzaExpress. If you could get into that restaurant on a Saturday night, we'd decide the area was no good,' he says. 'When people say, "I want to open a restaurant" it has to be led by location. You can have a great idea but you have to find somewhere it's going to work.' Market research is common sense, he says. 'It's about trying to understand what the people in an area want. You can easily alienate customers by putting in something they consider poncy.'

Roy Ellis and **Neil Macleod** went to Manchester to research locations for their first bar. In a town on the outskirts, they were 'served filthy, warm tomato juices by a temporary manager who had two black eyes. That made us a bit scared.' Leaving the bar, they noticed a stream of young people coming out of another bar. 'About fifty people came out and we thought it must be empty, but it wasn't – it was packed,' says Ellis. 'We said, "If we can't make money in this town, we won't be able to make any money at all." ' From there, they developed a strategy of buying and improving underperforming assets.

James Keay did 'a bit of test marketing' before leaving his job to start up a skip-hire company. 'I knew the main sectors that I was looking at, but I didn't put a great deal of thought into any of it – when you've got some customers, you need some suppliers, and so it goes on. I learned to crawl, walk and run all at the same time. If you've got a lot of self-belief, you just get on and do it.'

> **20/20** . . . 'People do use the phrase "right time, right place" but you're in the right place because you *put* yourself there and your PR is working.'
>
> – Sonita Alleyne

Getting a feel for the market may include spending time in a certain place – particularly if the plan is to launch abroad. **Scott Lyons** says that, as an American, he was naïve about coming to Britain to set up his business. 'If you're going to come from another country to start up, you need to understand the market, what you are doing and where you are going. We thought when we moved here permanently, there would be no problems, but things started to go wrong two days before we came, when our main investor went bankrupt, leaving us with little money.

'When we got here, all the contacts we had made acted very differently when we were in their territory. That first year was one of the biggest struggles of my life. We were living in Sheffield, because that was where our investor was, and felt like fish out of water. In New York City, after a meeting with someone, they call you back right away. Here, it was more of a game. I remember calling people and freaking out that they weren't calling back. My grand vision was to combine the two cultures and come out with a really interesting product but, with hindsight, we needed a year at least to understand what was going on.'

Research should help to define the characteristics of customers and the potential market position of a product, and to estimate sales, though **Jonathan Hartnell-Beavis** and **James Millar**, who spent time interviewing shoppers about their preferences before launching their business, tell a cautionary tale. 'I was sure that people would love to get their groceries delivered, and we asked a few hundred people what they thought,' says Hartnell-Beavis. 'About seventy per cent of them said they would use a grocery home-shopping service, so we were thinking, "Cripes, in a month's time we're going to explode." Of course, it doesn't work quite like that.'

Put another way, says Millar, the task seemed momentous. 'We had to think, "How do we convert the great mass of Londoners to buy food without seeing it from two blokes they've never heard of?"' They designed a catalogue and tested it stringently. 'We got my mum and Jonathan's to look at our catalogue from a feminine angle. They pulled out all the crisp packets and put in some real foods.'

> **20/20** . . . 'Try to get the support of your family but don't ask them about your business plan. Anything you say, they're going to say yes to. You've got to ask people that you've never met before to get a true response.'
> – Shawn Taylor

Statistics don't always provide the full story of a market's potential. The partners who set up the drinks company Innocent took unpaid leave from their jobs and devoted months to testing their product in their chosen market. 'In the summer of 1997 we bought £500 worth of fruit and put out two recycling bins at a jazz festival in southwest London,' says **Richard Reed**. 'One was labelled "yes", the other was "no". Our poster read, "Do you think we should give up our day jobs to make 'smoothies'?" – and at the end of the weekend the "yes" bin was full.'

'While we were still in our full-time jobs, we worked out a business plan and set ourselves various hurdles to judge whether we were going to really leave our jobs,' says his partner **Jon Wright**. 'The first was, "Is our product better than anyone else's?" The "yes" bin at the jazz festival was a great start in absolute terms but we weren't going to stop till the product was the best.'

They hoped to launch the drinks brand that September, but soon realised it would take longer. 'Everybody told us, "You need sugar and water" but it took time to discover that those are just for a manufacturer's convenience,' says Reed. 'We said we weren't going to take short cuts just to make a large profit or to make a million bottles which we could keep in a warehouse. We were paranoid about getting it right.'

Finally, the following May, four hundred cases of 'smoothie' drinks were ready for delivery. 'We sold three cases to the local shop where we'd been buying our sandwiches,' says Reed. 'That was on the Thursday. The whole business rested on twenty-four little bottles sat on that fridge shelf. We locked ourselves in the office and didn't come out till the end of Friday. We crept along to the shop but the window was high, so we had to pile bread crates to climb up and see there were only four bottles left – we had sold twenty bottles in a day and a half! It actually could work. We didn't relax, but the paranoia eased.'

Alex van Someren and his brother **Nicko** flew to San Francisco in 1996 to find out about other encryption products at a data security conference. 'It was very revealing – there were people doing hardware but nobody doing accelerated hardware for speeding up encryption,' says Alex. 'There was a big opportunity, but nobody seemed to be doing what we were proposing to do. The need was one that we saw very clearly – however, nobody else saw the need. So it was like "Are we crazy or is it just that we are smarter than everyone else?" Venture capitalists prefer it when you have a competitor, because it shows you're not crazy. As it turned out, there was a public company worth hundreds of millions doing a similar thing.'

20/20 . . . 'Spend lots of time researching in order to work out a compelling proposition for your target audience.'

– Maziar Darvish

New skills

Many first-time entrepreneurs realise that they need to seek training and advice before venturing into business. **Charlotte Barker** enrolled on a five-month part-time business course. 'It was the first rung of the ladder, but it gave me an overview. Self-awareness is so important, to broaden your net, and to think about what you are doing and why,' says Barker. She then persuaded the marketing department of a local university to provide data for her business plan, and researched and corresponded with other entrepreneurs through the Internet.

Barker also signed up for a pilot mentoring programme run by the Glasgow Development Agency and was matched with a senior executive at Marks & Spencer. 'I requested someone from a retail background because I didn't have a clue about how that worked. We only met a dozen times but it was really useful to go through everything, and my mentor had the address book and was able to introduce me to other people,' she says.

The exercise also helped her to work through a 'critical inch' list. 'The list was what I needed to get through every day in order to get the business moving forward to each new stage. There's only so much you can get through but, if you can get through the key things, they will catapult you forward into the next stage.'

Amy Carroll learned from an early experience to be choosy about advisers. 'A lot of advice we've had hasn't been very apposite to the business. Our accountant told us that we should buy the building we were working in [and] we were convinced it would provide us with income in the future, but we bought the building at the height of the property boom and, when we wanted to move out because our business was expanding, we couldn't get rid of it. Prices had crashed, but by then we'd grown from a handful of people to fifty. The upshot was that we sold the building several years later, at a loss, after numerous problems with tenants and a squatter. It was always a negative feature on our balance sheet.'

20/20 . . . 'It's often the toughest advice which is the easiest to follow if it's right.'

– Angela Mortimer

As nineteen-year-olds, **Simon Needham** and **James Sommerville** went to each department of the companies they worked for and quizzed colleagues. 'We didn't have a clue about business – we were complete and utter virgins at the whole thing,' they admit. 'Initially I went around the office that I was working in and literally said to people, "How does printing work? What do you do there?"' says Needham. 'I asked some questions and I was able to use their answers as a basis. It wasn't magic.'

Arthur and **Irene Allen** initially turned to their local bank for help. 'When we first started, we were pretty hazy about where our customers would be. We didn't have the foggiest about business, so we asked everywhere for advice. In a local bank, we spotted a notice saying STARTING A BUSINESS? FREE ADVICE, so we made an appointment and brought along this business plan, which we'd spent hours sharpening. It was a pretty folksy document. After an hour, the guy stood up and said, "Thanks very much. I've got another meeting now and I have to advise you that the bank will be unable to offer you any overdraft facilities whatsoever." That was the sum total of the advice.'

20/20 . . . 'Find good advisers – lawyers and accountants. They don't need to be the most expensive.'

– William Harris

Jonathan Elvidge began to read business books when he moved from a technical role into a sales role, before starting his own business. 'I'd done no professional selling but I started reading books about successful salespeople. You can absorb technique pretty quickly, and what I used to do when I had finished [a book] was to write a list of ten things that I felt were particularly strong.' Elvidge also began to read popular psychology books and says that this shaped his development as an entrepreneur. 'I began to see parallels in these books: things like "pray for what you want" and "if you believe, it will happen". Salespeople would say you have to visualise your goals, and focus on ways you could achieve those goals. I used to believe that, in order to do something well, you had to have a natural talent in that area. From reading books, I learned that wasn't true.'

> **20/20** . . . 'Success in business is not a reflection of the intelligence of an individual, but of drive, motivation and clear focus.'
>
> – Jonathan Elvidge

Advice, training and mentoring are not an investment solely for first-time entrepreneurs. **Barry Bester** still finds it helpful to discuss strategies with another experienced retail entrepreneur, **Julian Richer**. 'One of the biggest influences on me has been Julian. He's been helping us with customer service for a while, every couple of months. It's not so much about learning new things: it's really about going back over the things that we already know.'

As a teenager, **Charlie Muirhead** 'worked every single opportunity' and went on after school to work for a pro-audio hire company before college, and start his own company. **Alex van Someren** worked for the Cambridge computer firm Acorn as a teenager. 'By the time Alex left school in 1982, he had an address book full of the names of some of the most influential people in the computer industry. We both got a deep technical understanding and became used to dealing with people in the industry,' says his brother **Nicko**, who also worked for Acorn.

> **20/20** . . . 'Most people going into business don't truly understand it and that's where the problems start.'
>
> – Colin Halpern

Nick Austin says he got invaluable experience from running someone else's company before founding his own. 'We learned a set of principles in that period in which we ran Matchbox, so that, when we finally cut ourselves adrift, we were so far up the learning curve that we didn't make serious errors that set us back. Everyone talks about strategy, and strategy is really important, but we have seen great companies with wonderful strategies kill themselves because there's nobody managing the detail.'

Writing the plan

Coupled with the ability to instil confidence, a business plan is a useful tool for presenting a proposal to potential investors or lenders.

The plan includes research and projections, and some people write two plans – one for investors, one as an internal growth charter.

> **20/20 . . .** 'When we saw something, we knew what we could sell it for and we knew there was a market. A lot of people had overlooked this.'
>
> – Juliana Galvin

Sue Welland wrote a business plan when seeking venture capital to grow Future Forests. 'Originally we used some business students to help us write it, but they just couldn't. You must always write it well, and always write it yourself. You might need to get outside help, but take that as part of a learning process. Writing a plan is not just to get capital into the business: it also helps you grow. You mustn't underestimate the amount of time it takes to do it and get the funding you need. We started talking to venture capitalists in November, finished writing the plan in March and got the funding in July.'

Rob Lewis and **Anna Russell** spent months working on a business plan before launching Silicon.com. 'We talked about our plan so much that we knew exactly what we wanted to do,' says Russell. 'We spent a lot of time refining it, and we went through about five business plans before we went out and got investment. You really have to test the market, test revenue propositions and business models, and prove the concept if you have the cash available. You can spend forever dithering and not actually doing anything, but I would recommend that you test the proposition as quickly as possible, within a sensible set of structures.'

Mark Dixon advises: 'Spend as much time as possible working on your original plan and review the plan regularly: once a week or once a month at the beginning, continually reviewing the business's activities. Speak to your team and also your customers as much as possible so that you really understand what makes the business tick and then, persistently and relentlessly, review the business model. Never allow complacency to enter your business arena.'

> **20/20 . . .** 'It's a little bit chicken and egg with your business plan. You set a target to spend and it's tempting to spend more.'
>
> – Nick Rose

One calculation to build into the plan is the projected price of products or services. 'What we did was to look and see what other people were doing,' says **Barry Bester**. 'There was a company up in Manchester who were doing slightly different pricing and we tweaked that and used it.' Not every entrepreneur bases price on costs of production. 'I have never ever looked at what it cost us to make the product,' says **Simon Notley**. 'The cost is totally irrelevant. I have always priced the product on my gut feeling as to what I thought we could get for it. As a result, our margins are fairly good. If a bed cost us £100 to make and we sell it for £500, I have to say that that's been crucial to our success.'

Underpricing can have drastic effects, as **Alex Shipp** describes. 'We designed a virus scanner – at first we had quite a lot of success, but one day we discovered our main competitors were selling their version for a lot more money. We couldn't match them in price. It was a massive miscalculation: we were selling the system for £1,000 but they were selling for £40,000. We quickly realised our potential customers thought their version must be better because the price was higher. We were selling to small companies but bigger companies didn't want to know. They wanted to buy from someone with a bigger name. We were trying to break into the market for a couple of years but never quite did it.'

For **Nick Austin**, whose business, Vivid Imaginations, imports and sells toys, costs and prices are very tightly related. 'We have occasionally underpriced certain products and at the end of the year, after you've spent on advertising and everything else, you suddenly realise you're losing money on the product because your price is wrong. I've seen more companies go bust in this industry from underpricing than from any other reason. People take a view that, if they underprice, the product will go out at a cheaper price and, instead of selling a hundred, will sell millions. It doesn't work that way. Retailers are telling you, "If you put your prices up we're not stocking it any more." Suddenly you're trapped in a situation where you're running a low-margin business. You have to get it absolutely right. If it's too low you don't make any money.'

When exchange rates changed, costs for Vivid went up by as much as 15 per cent. 'If we hadn't reacted and moved our prices up and changed our products so that we could "hide" the cost increases, we would have been in trouble. If you take product X off the market and replace it with product Y – this is where the constant reinvention comes in – that redevelopment sometimes allows you to manoeuvre around those problems.'

20/20 . . . 'The trick with pricing is to have a spread of things. We also spend a lot of time reading about where everyone else thinks we are in the market.'

– Mark Constantine

Martin Rutty and **Tim Gilbert** staved off the effects of recession in the early nineties by raising prices. 'You can pitch yourself at the cheap and cheerful end of the market and there's nothing wrong with that, but you've got to make sure it's absolutely no-frills whatsoever,' says Rutty. 'If you go for the top end of a market, you must offer more than your nearest competitor – something better, more innovative, perhaps slightly lateral. That offering changes all the time. Eleven or twelve years ago, we were offering smart couriers and reliability – couriers who weren't covered in grease, had a smart, newish van and had been given some training. It's the norm now, but back then it was a new thing.

Gail Federici and **John Frieda** carved a new price niche in the early nineties. '[More than] ten years ago, we launched Frizz-Ease . . . it was a different product, and it required education,' says Federici. 'To compete against multibillion-dollar companies, we had to rely on our salon heritage, to come up with products that were prescriptive, with a compelling proposition that really performed. The most difficult thing was to convince people to go against the conventional price range, and we insisted that products had to be displayed separately so that customers could see the "before" and "after" effect. John also demonstrated the products on television, and that was key.'

A business plan should also define how a product will get to market. **Simon Notley** initially wanted to sell beds to other shops rather than directly to the public, 'but in hindsight, that would have been a disaster because they would all have wanted thirty days' credit and, with the small amount of capital we had, we wouldn't have been able to finance that'. **Neil Franklin** says that businesses selling to other businesses must decide early on whether to supply or partner. 'If you supply, you are a middleman, an agent, a broker; if you partner, you can supply it so much better, because you are following that company's strategic development. There's a market for both supplier and partner – you just have to discover naturally which is for you, where you feel comfortable.'

20/20 . . . 'In business you need the thickest skin in the world, but thick skin is no good without strategy.'

– Neil Franklin

A business plan must be flexible enough to adapt to changing circumstances, particularly in a fast-growing market. 'Almost every company I see started off with one business plan and ends up with something related but different,' says **Charlie Muirhead**. 'That's not accidental – it's very hard to hypothesise when you're addressing a new opportunity in a market which isn't yet there.' What you don't choose to do is at least as important as what you do choose, says **Alex van Someren**. 'It's about evaluating variables and making an educated guess. Risk taking is about being prepared to make a very quick judgment based on insufficient data about what to do next – and it distinguishes those who are true entrepreneurs.'

QUESTIONS FROM THE EDGE

How should I go about researching my market?

Terry Pullen: 'Consider why people will choose you as a service or as a product. Then test that out. My university-of-life attitude to market research is to ask the people who you think will buy the product or service off you. You can never ask too many of them.'

Neil Franklin: 'Look at potential clients. Read their financial reports, saying, "Where are they going? What's their core business? What's their strategy? How are they trying to align themselves to the marketplace? What's their key message?" You have to build understanding from a very low platform. Ask the obvious. Badger the life out of the client's marketing department.'

How did you set your prices?

Adam Twiss: 'Our prices were largely set by the competition and that has guided our pricing, even now. I guess the key thing to understand is the benefits that you bring to the customer. You need to make sure that the price point is such that you get the right decision makers on board easily. A lot of our stuff in the early days was priced at £1,000 – we were selling to technical people who could spend that amount because it was within the size of a credit-card budget.'

Nick Austin: 'You have to research your market really well because if you underprice your goods, you make it very difficult to move the price up. If you overprice you will not end up with any business. You have to do a lot of research to get it right in the micro-detail. You need a very strong feeling for what the consumer will pay for certain classes of product. The relation between price and cost is very complex and sensitive and I think it's really important to understand all of that. If you get it wrong it has serious consequences.'

What were your worries before you launched?

Robin Hutson: 'There was a lot to think about so failure didn't really come into my mind. Then, a couple of days before we opened, when we had spent every penny we had available and more, and my house was on the line as a guarantee for the business, Gerard [Basset] and I were having a cup of coffee and I thought, "If no one comes, what the hell do we do?" There was no contingency plan and the panic came only because I had stopped to consider. When we opened the hotel doors, that feeling disappeared.'

Liz Meston: 'We were so worried that someone was going to do it before us. I remember waking up in the middle of the night saying to myself, "I want to be there first." '

What advice would you offer me before launch?

Philip Newton: 'Nothing is ever as good or as bad as it first appears and so almost every problem can be overcome, provided you believe in [your idea] in the first place.'

Andrew Pollock: 'If you make wrong decisions, don't agonise over them. Stop, and do something else. It's not the good decisions that count: it's how you react to bad decisions.'

James Sommerville: 'Knowing where you want to go is really important. Make it a screensaver and don't forget it. If it's just kind of fuzzy, you're likely to hang around the same area. We always had definite ideas: "In two years' time we are going to be doing this." Having a plan drives you to the next level. If you say, "By the time I'm twenty-eight we will have an office in Paris" you have a much better chance than saying, "One day I wish I could have an office in France." '

Charles Falzon: 'Stick with your vision, be prepared for hard work, and above all do not fear the risk of failure. Persistence and commitment will pay off.'

Neil Franklin: 'Make sure you understand what you're trying to achieve. Get your people in place. Cover all the business disciplines even if at first you end up doing four or five of them yourself. Get the best finance manger you can.'

Brian Clivaz: 'Have a clear vision. Write it down in as much detail as possible. Take advice from people you admire and whose judgment you respect. Seek out those who have already achieved and ask their advice. Listen to the advice of experts and then go back to your plan and rewrite it. Believe in yourself and your ability to achieve your end vision and then go for it. Don't give up. It will be far more difficult than you first imagined, but hold on to that original vision with the tenacity of a bulldog and don't give in.'

ASSESS FOUR

- Research is essential: it should define characteristics of your customers, why they will buy and how much you can sell
- A test run may help to refine the product or service
- Don't let research delay execution unnecessarily
- Don't stop researching once you've started up

- Use Paul Barrow's *The Best-Laid Business Plans: How to Write Them, How to Pitch Them* (Virgin), to draft your plan
- Think carefully about how prices relate to costs. Underpricing does not mean you will sell more
- Define your route to market
- Clearly assess risks
- Refine your business plan before looking for investment
- Time invested in training may help to avoid mistakes
- Nothing beats in-depth experience

Quick list: In fewer than ten words, describe

- The characteristics of your customer
- What sets your product apart from other suppliers
- What needs your product will meet in your customer
- What factors will affect whether your customer buys
- The current and possible future trends in the market
- How long it will take you to get established in the market
- How much of the market you plan to take in the long term
- How you will price your products in the short to medium term
- The route via which you will sell your product or service
- What your overheads will be and what they will cost you
- When you will make sales, and how many
- When you will make a profit, and how much
- Whether and when you will need to raise money
- How you will support yourself during the start-up phase
- The elements of starting up that most concern you

Most businesses need cash for working capital and setting up costs, and a business plan should forecast the amount needed. Which is preferable, to borrow money or sell shares (equity)? Are friends and family good lenders? What kinds of start-ups do venture capitalists invest in? What other methods can be used to raise money?

Do it yourself

People who start businesses will usually have to invest in them personally, and some rely solely on their savings and cash flow for the first months or years. **Jez Nelson** and **Sonita Alleyne** each put £500 into a company bank account, and rented their first office above a kebab shop in Camden. 'There was no way we could survive by making radio programmes for independent stations, but Sonita had been involved in promoting concerts so we put on club nights to get cash in,' says Nelson.

Mike Altendorf and **Richard Thwaite** decided to apply for an overdraft, but the bank manager told them their plans were too ambitious. So they used credit cards, each borrowing up to £10,000 to start Conchango.

> **20/20** . . . 'We were careful not to raise money too early. It sharpens your focus when it's your own money, but it sharpens your focus even more when it's someone else's.'
> – Lynn Forester

Kevin Bulmer was also unable to obtain an overdraft facility, and went the same route – he and Kate Copestake pushed their credit cards to the limit for their first six months. 'Looking back, it was either astonishingly brave or ridiculously stupid,' he says. 'I'd just left employment as a graphic designer and was just starting to build up a portfolio of clients. There was no proven turnover and we had no assets against which to raise money. Neither Kate nor I had formerly run a business. All of our family and friends were in employment, so it was a complete new venture for us. And the one area where common sense did go out of the window was funding.

'We were being showered with credit-card offers – so, just to see what would happen, we took a few of them up. We filled everything out completely honestly; we didn't lie or fabricate any information. The only common denominator was the question, "Have you borrowed money for a mortgage?" They didn't ask if you had any other credit cards. We secured all these cards and gradually started to use them to buy things: I think I had about eight at one stage. We were very cautious and it was a facility that allowed us to ease our cash flow, as people were paying late. We were able to pay them all off within two years and we didn't get to a huge amount, but we could have gone mad.'

20/20 . . . 'I've put my house on the line all the time. I've always put everything into what I have believed in, and I've lost a few houses. I always used to spend more than I earned, so I got myself into debt and financial problems and had to start again.'

– Neil Franklin

To start Listawood, **Arthur** and **Irene Allen** borrowed money from their families, invested a few hundred pounds of their own, and eventually negotiated a small overdraft. They also signed up for the government's enterprise allowance scheme, which paid them £50 a week each for their first six months in business. They didn't go so far as to put their house on the line, but their kitchen became a casualty. 'We had no proper roof on it for years,' explains Arthur. 'We had started to renovate [but] it didn't get fixed for five years because we either had no money or were simply too busy. I used to like it when winter came and it snowed – at least then our house looked the same as everyone else's!'

Family, friends and acquaintances

Social and business contacts are potential investors. **David Landau** raised money to start *Loot* by selling shares to friends and family. 'We ran through that money pretty quickly and raised more through family and friends till we reached the point where we had almost made it. The investors were my sister and brother-in-law and friends, people I'd known for many years and had done other things with. The fact that your family and closest friends are putting money into your business is an incentive to some degree, because you feel doubly responsible and that focuses your mind, but in reality with any money you take, unless you are very ruthless, you make sure that you don't lose it.'

Mark Jackson raised initial funding for Helphire by persuading a friend who was a dentist – and his clients – to invest. 'We were well capitalised,' says **Michael Symons**. 'That was an example of Mark's self-confidence – he went up to people and said, "I've got a nice idea, give me £10,000 and don't ask any questions. Just let us get on with it." You wouldn't think that approach would work, but sufficient people had faith in him.' The pair raised £160,000 from sixteen investors and avoided borrowing from the bank until eighteen months after launch.

> **20/20** . . . 'When we were looking for seed capital, we had people queuing up to give us money and I remember thinking, "Well, we can get the money from anyone. It's not a matter of how much, but do we like the people involved? What are they going to add to our business?" '
>
> – Anna Russell

Loans and grants

Often entrepreneurs finance their businesses through a number of sources. Most banks offer short-term loans but for some businesses these are less than ideal: not every entrepreneur can secure a loan; amounts lent may be limited; and a loan can be called in at short notice.

A track record in business and the backing of other investors may give a head start. **Nick Austin** and **Alan Bennie** borrowed £300,000 from the bank after matching it with the same amount they raised themselves. **Andrew Pollock** and **Simon Rees** also invested their own savings and persuaded the bank to lend them money. 'The bank took a big punt but we said, "You've known us as partners at Ernst & Young. What's changed?" We had no security, but they lent us £300,000 and we had a £100,000 professional practice loan from 3i.'

20/20 . . . 'Learning the ability to be not too polite has been important. I've learned it just by coming out of meetings and going, "Oh, God, I should have said that" – and realising I didn't say something because it was impolite, the etiquette of meetings and all that. I've learned to just not worry about it and say, "This is what I want." '

– Sonita Alleyne

Will King raised initial funds from family and friends, and took out personal loans to support himself. 'We got £30,000 over two years from shareholders, including my dad and Herbie's. At that time the amounts we needed – although they were so tiny – seemed huge, and access to money at that point was rubbish. My wife Ann and I worked together on the business for the first four months and it was completely untenable. We had no money and were paying to get sales of the product, so she went back to work.'

Then King sold his first shaving product into a big retail chain, and realised the business needed another injection of cash to expand. He went to the bank for a loan after he had been in business for two years. 'When Boots and Harrods took the product, although the business was still tiny, it was the beginnings of something big,' says **Herbie Dayal**. 'There were real customers and there was a lot to do.' King remembers how Dayal saw he needed an extra pair of hands, but was concerned about finances. 'Herbie and I sat in a pub one day and he saw I couldn't cope with running the business from home and getting deliveries to Boots with couriers. He said, "How can you pay for my wife and kids?" It had to be done properly.' The pair borrowed substantial funds from their bank in three instalments under the government's loan guarantee scheme, designed to enable small businesses without sufficient security to raise money for growth.

Jonathan Elvidge secured an overdraft facility using his house as security. He planned to open his first shop in time for Christmas, but then discovered that the finish date for the new shopping complex in which it was located had moved back from November to March. 'When it became clear that Princes Quay wasn't going to be ready in November, the potential Christmas sales disappeared,' he says. 'I was guessing at costs to a huge extent but, even with the most optimistic forecasts, it was clear that I would need £20,000 more than I had already raised. The guy from the bank who agreed the overdraft called and said, "Look, we can't agree this funding – we've got no security. We know what we've offered isn't going to be enough."

'That was a really difficult time and if someone had said to me, "OK, it can't be done, and you have the option to get your job back," I would have gladly done it. I'd already spent the money I had available, about £2,000, on stationery costs and market research, which included paying a student £300 to get some of his friends involved so that I could prove I'd done market research in the local area and build that into the business plan. I also needed the funds to be proven by a set of reasonable accounts, which cost about £1,000 and which I remember thinking was an enormous figure. I knew that without having someone to approve a big page of numbers, it wasn't going to happen.'

Elvidge could see his potential business sinking before his eyes. Help came in the form of a case study. 'I remembered reading about Sophie Mirman, who started Sock Shop, and I dug out information that referred to her early days and talked about her getting support from the small firms loan guarantee scheme. I just happened to fit all the criteria – I had an idea that people supported but I didn't have the security to raise the extra finance I needed, so I went to my bank and said, "What about this?" '

Under the scheme, the Department of Trade and Industry provides security by guaranteeing the majority of the loan (up to 85 per cent for businesses that have been running for more than two years). 'That was how the money was raised,' says Elvidge. 'Without it, I would have been lost and in a situation of personal bankruptcy before the shop even happened.' Elvidge was then offered investment by his future business partner, **Andrew Hobbs**, but at that stage turned it down. 'By then I'd raised money with the help of the loan scheme. Having spent the best part of two years struggling, you feel like you don't ever want to let it go.'

Shawn Taylor also struggled financially as he was setting up his first service centre. He believed he had £5,000 backing: a £2,500 loan from the Prince's Trust and the same amount from a local council. However, it transpired that, although the business premises were within the council's catchment area, Taylor did not qualify for the grant because he lived five miles outside it. 'I was just about to open the doors when the money was pulled,' he says.

'The trouble was that I needed a ramp to lift the cars, and that cost £2,490. I thought, "That's OK" because I was told I could lease it. An hour after the money was pulled, I got a phone call from the ramp people saying, "Because you're a new business, we can't lease the ramp to you; you'll have to buy it." I didn't have any other money to put down as a guarantee so I had to buy the ramp. I was left with about £10. My fiancée had lent me £2,000 to do the place up and I'd spent that already. I thought to myself, "I've got to go with it. I can't do anything else." It wasn't a nice feeling but I'd sacrificed everything for this and there was no way I was pulling out.'

Kevin Bulmer warns new entrepreneurs to be careful when looking to borrow, even from apparently reliable sources. 'When we started, there were a lot of new organisations which promised to make government funding available for businesses which were training people. We got involved with one organisation, set up to distribute money to worthwhile businesses. We dealt with these people for eighteen months and paid for them to look at our accounts and consider us for funding. We wasted months of time, and no money was forthcoming. From that experience and others, we learned that raising funds can be a minefield because there are a lot of people who make money out of those people who are trying to *raise* money. We paid for research on investors . . . we put adverts in various publications that purported to be specialists. But we could ill afford to support this strange little group of parasites.'

Business angels and venture capital

Business angels look to invest on an individual basis in a venture that appears promising. Like **Charlie Muirhead**, they have often been entrepreneurs themselves. Muirhead borrowed £20,000 from a family friend to start Orchestream and funded its progress using fees from his own consultancy work. He also persuaded Hermann Hauser and

Esther Dyson to invest in the company and later went on to co-found an angel network, i-Gabriel. 'At the end of 1999 I was beginning to talk to a number of entrepreneurs who came to me for advice,' he says. 'Call it deal flow – there were a lot of calls coming in. I wanted to be able to offer advice, the usual kind of thing, so I helped a handful of people and soon realised there was an opportunity to invest some money. I didn't have any so I set up a group of people that could pull some funds together. I saw there was a big gap in the UK for smart technology angel investment in the sub-$1 million bracket.'

Jon Wright and his colleagues at the drinks company Innocent found a business angel shortly after launching their business. 'We kept running out of money,' says Wright. 'At first, we were producing more drinks than we sold. We'd be there in Regent's Park on a sunny afternoon handing it out for free. If we sold stuff fast, we ran out of money. If we didn't sell, we lost money. We realised that we were going to have to find a few hundred thousand pounds, but no bank would get involved with guys who were trundling around London to sell juice to sandwich shops. To them, it probably seemed a bit too ordinary.'

'We had this naïve view which figured we would leave our jobs and sell juice, and use the money to buy more juice,' adds **Richard Reed**. 'Turns out that wasn't a great way. You need your office, all these things that require money. We realised we were going to need some money to do a better job sooner. As a new business you've got two options for getting money. One is to borrow the money and incur debt. The other is venture capital money, so you sell equity. Because we had very few assets and were untried and untested, it was impossible to get a start-up loan, so we went out into the market to try to raise money from a venture capitalist or business angel.

'The business angel we eventually went with came up through a contact. Things moved really quickly with him. It was just like going for a job interview or a first date – you know when it's working, because it felt so right on both sides of the table. Our business angel spent three hours grilling us about when we were going to get married, and where we wanted to go in life. It was like, "I'm going to invest in you and I don't know anything about you." It's a common theory that at that stage you're buying the people and their CVs, but our angel really bought the idea and put his trust in us as people to deliver it. The relationship has been fantastic.'

Nick Rose and **Jordan Mayo** were sought out by their first angel. 'Our venture had been covered in a national newspaper and he had a keen interest in education, so he put the first amount of money up. As plans developed we went out to a few high-net-worth individuals, who were really looking at whether to invest in us as people. In fundraising the key things to get across are your own competency and passion.'

Adam Twiss and **Damian Reeves** attracted funding from a number of investors. 'It happened by chance that we found angel investors. We met people in their professional capacity who wanted to invest on a personal level,' says Twiss. 'The advantage of having twenty or so angel investors was that we got access to twenty people's networks. The flip side is that angel investors are often hobby investors and, when they're interested, perhaps they're too interested and there's a danger that they want to meddle too much; but, when they're busy with their day jobs, they're not necessarily there to help you.'

20/20 . . . 'Entrepreneurs are rarely successful in a vacuum. The best entrepreneurs have to be visionary but they also have to be collaborative. Don't think that you can surround yourself with yes men and take on the world yourself. Don't believe that you know better than everyone working for you. You need to exploit every contact you have and every contact your contacts have. You need to build a network and develop as many partnerships as possible.'

– Stewart Dodd

It has to be said that venture capital is not a funding route suitable for many start-ups. In general, venture capitalists invest in companies operating in fast-growing or large markets, and look for experienced management, evidence that profits will materialise, a sizable return and often a rapid exit. As one seasoned entrepreneur puts it, 'If you are doing well, you don't hear from them. If you are not doing well, they are all over you like a rash.' Entrepreneurs seeking funds from venture capitalists will, in addition to their own due-diligence costs, be required to pay for legal and professional fees for the deal, and possibly to seek partners or form a consortium of investors.

Andy Kitchener remembers, 'I made the mistake of wasting time trying to sell my idea to venture capitalists who had little understanding of what it was about. We had a prototype working, and had put in the best part of £150,000 ourselves. We were advised to seek £2.2 million from venture capitalists, and we had four directors, each of whom went to nine meetings. In each case, they spent a day preparing for it. That took three months, and the venture capitalists said, "Yes, we're very interested. Just cross the finishing line, then we'll put more money in." We got nothing from them – they wanted us to prove we'd got to the stage where we didn't need them.'

For **Carol Dukes**, venture capital was the right option when she was starting up ThinkNatural. 'If you want to raise money but can't raise loans against something because you have nothing to secure it against, you have got to either know people with money or go to people with venture capital money,' she says. 'I didn't really think about looking for a business angel, because of the new availability of venture capital [in the late nineties] and it was an advantage having professional investors involved. Business angels can be wonderful or they can be awful, and it's somehow much more based on personality, whereas, if you have a company investing in you, obviously they can be bad, but they won't usually be completely barking mad.'

Dukes began by talking to a friend who worked at a corporate finance boutique and who introduced her to Amadeus Capital Partners. Four months later, Dukes and her partner **Emma Crowe** had secured £2.4 million from Amadeus and other investors in order to start their company. 'We had both been in the Internet industry for so long that we could call up old friends and people knew that we had delivered before,' says Crowe. 'Once you've done a good deal two or three times, it cuts down the negotiations to a tenth of the time.'

The pair raised a further £10 million in 2000 from their existing investors and others, including Kingfisher. Dukes says raising that amount of money was tough in the prevailing climate but adds, 'Even though we had hardly been trading at that point, we could show we had done everything we'd said we would do, on budget and on time.'

Alex and **Nicko van Someren** ran several ventures together before meeting a venture capitalist who offered to invest in their next project. 'These days most people go out and look for a venture capitalist but we were much luckier,' says Alex. 'We have all the wrong history because a venture capitalist walked into our path and offered funding for any idea that we had. Nicko literally met this guy at a dinner party and came back saying, "Alex, Alex, I've found the money. What should we do?" It was a back-to-front kind of story.'

The brothers were running a company with other partners at the time, and proposed that the venture capital firm invest in their existing business. 'They told us they really only wanted to invest in new businesses. Venture capitalists want more equity,' says Alex. 'We had a very difficult dinner with our co-founders and said, "It's like this – we want to go this way and you are going to have to be prepared to put up with seeing us go." I mean, if someone offered us £1 million why wouldn't we take the opportunity?'

20/20 . . . 'Nobody comes to an entrepreneur and says, "Here's £2 million, go off and do it." Entrepreneurs have to commit themselves, knowing nobody is going to support them.'

– Alec Crawford

Other means

Some entrepreneurs use existing business or skills to provide funds to start a new venture. In the mid-seventies, **David Rhodes** began doing research to develop products for the Tornado aircraft and components for electronic warfare. Needing some capital, he wrote software for communication satellites and sold it to companies in order to buy the equipment so that he could develop prototypes for his newly formed company Filtronic.

20/20 . . . 'The business took off like a rocket. The only shock was discovering how much tax we owed.'

– Angela Mortimer

Robin Hutson and **Gerard Basset** raised £500,000 from private investors to buy their first hotel in Winchester. 'I went to friends and relatives first and scraped together a little bit,' says Hutson. 'One thing leads to another. Someone would say "Have you tried so-and-so?" We were lucky to get funding from the Royal Bank of Scotland early on but I told a slight white lie when I said I had a commitment of £500,000 from other shareholders. They said if I produced that, they would back it up with debt of £750,000. That meant I could go and tell the other shareholders – it was a bit of a chicken-and-egg scenario.'

For working capital, they came up with the idea of asking wine companies to sponsor bedrooms. 'We raised £60,000 in sponsorship and this was very useful, the best sort of money – there was no interest and no shares at stake. Another entrepreneur had set up a country house hotel in Leicestershire and managed to get sponsorship from a diverse range of companies. I'd always thought the idea was pretty neat so, when we started to talk about names for the hotel, I said we could call the bedrooms after famous châteaux. That led to "Let's have sponsored rooms." Early on it gave journalists something to write about and endeared us to the wine trade.'

QUESTIONS FROM THE EDGE

What should be my initial calculations when thinking about how to finance my new business?

Terry Pullen: 'The first thing to consider is how much money you need. Add that amount to the first figure that you think there's no way you could ever overspend by, and then double that figure. Then, maybe, you are about right. You also need to consider how much money you need to take from other people, and how much you're going to spend in order to take that money. That will define your business and your profitability. You can't generalise about how long it will take to be profitable, but you need to not lie to yourself. An entrepreneur who is on his own will tend to lie to himself – you don't think you're doing it, but you will underestimate costs and overestimate your turnover.'

Why should I ask my family and friends for money?

James Millar: 'I have to recommend going to your family and friends for support, because I think this is really all about confidence. If you can gain some confidence because your dad, your mum or your mate has sufficient confidence to give you some money, that's got to be a good move. If you lose it, that's when you've got to start behaving like a man. You may face a firing squad, you may have to face them every Christmas – but that's good. That's the hold you have, and it's almost an incentive.'

How did you raise working capital?

Robyn Jones: 'I was very cheeky. I approached clients to pay a twelfth of the cost upfront as working capital, but in reality we didn't pay the staff or suppliers until the end of the month. That meant I was able to self-fund the business.'

Charlotte Barker: 'I had a Morris Traveller car called Harold, and I sold that to pay for the first print run of my game. I got £3,500 for the car. You've got to sacrifice things to get things moving.'

Who are the best investors to choose?

Neil Franklin: 'Investors who think like you. All investors want a return on their investment, but at what cost? It's vital that your investment partner understands what you're trying to do and, if not, find another one. Don't be frightened to call the shots – you're offering this guy an opportunity.'

Did you draw a salary to start with?

Howard Leigh: 'My partner Hugo [Haddon-Grant] and I committed to each other that we wouldn't draw a salary for a year. We each put in £10,000. I think it's a good way to focus your mind on what you're doing, to say, "Right, I will have to live off my life savings for a year." It impressed the bank manager much more . . . and it was tax-effective. In fact we generated sufficient funds to draw salaries after ten months.'

How much equity should I sell?

Richard Reed: 'Giving away equity is obviously the most expensive thing you're ever going to do. You've got to be really careful about how much you release. The thing that I found most surprising is that there are no rules. It's a pure economic negotiation: how much do you want, how much is the investor prepared to give you? You can pitch something and get laughed out of a room or you can have people thinking they're getting a steal. Don't give a lot of equity away at first – you'll pretty soon need some more money in.'

Alex van Someren: 'We ended up owning only ten per cent of the company, but it went on to be worth more than £100 million, so how can I complain? I never lost any sleep over the thought that I've been ripped off. It's a balancing act. If you can make a company successful, it doesn't matter. If you have a hundred per cent ownership of a dismal failure, it means nothing.'

I haven't been able to raise money – can I still succeed?

Mark Constantine: 'We had small overheads when we started Lush. The advantage of having no money was that the business had to be profitable. You have to generate your own cash. You have to get business. If you have a large sum of money behind you, it's not always a good thing. We only had a few bob between us but we did car boot sales to run up business and get started.'

How often should I communicate with investors?

Terry Pullen: 'Communication with investors and shareholders is crucial. The important thing is to get everything up front. Tell your investors, "This is the information you will receive and this is when you will receive it. Is that OK?" – whether that's giving them the annual accounts and asking them to the AGM, or giving them management information on a monthly basis.'

What are your reasons for avoiding venture capital funding?

Robyn Jones: 'We feel very much that, as soon as we go down a venture capital route, we won't be in control of our own destiny. You've got to give the venture capitalists the return, because they are going to want it. For us, the growth has always been there, so there's been no need to do it.'

What's your advice on seeking venture capital?

Carol Dukes: 'Work on the business plan. Make sure you understand it and have thought it through and apply common sense down the line. Talk to other people in the market, which is not something you can research in the library. Most venture capitalists, if they are serious, will give you access to other investees. These people won't usually say, "My investor is crap" but you can ask questions and assess areas of strength and weakness. Are they coming to the close of their fund, and looking for a quick payback? Have they just raised the money and now have a five-year horizon? What are they looking for, what are their expectations? Can they give you examples of companies that have run into difficulties, and what was their response? It's like meeting anyone new: you ask about where they are headed in their life.'

Alex van Someren: 'The more investing you do yourself, the more of the work you've done, the better the deal you're going to get. That's the single most important message for people to get because . . . if you throw yourself into a venture capitalist's hands, you will absolutely get fleeced. That's just how it is. If you are prepared to work hard and build up the business, it'll take you to a better level . . . venture capitalists want to own as much of your company as possible so you can't be too bothered about how much you own.'

I'm not very experienced in financial matters – any advice?

Will King: 'There are certain jobs that people just don't want to do, and for me that includes money management. It might be easy to dump the job on the accountant, but there are potential issues because you won't have any knowledge of the dynamics of funding your business. You've got to go and sell what you're doing first, rather than just gearing up to do it. No one's going to just give you the money.'

Ben Finn: 'Get an accountant and bookkeeper early on; get a financial manager in due course. It's a false economy spending time on things like this yourself, particularly if you haven't done them before.'

Anna Russell: 'Without question, you need to have someone on board who is a qualified accountant or has those skills. It's essential for any business, but particularly for a young business, to have someone that's going to have an iron fist when it comes to managing your cash flow.'

Terry Pullen: 'I would probably never set up a business again without getting in an industry-experienced financial controller. You may not be able to justify hiring a fully qualified financial director but you could hire that person for one day a week. Your business should afford that.'

Sonita Alleyne: 'Always try to get on with your bank manager. He's part of your company, so keep him informed about what you are doing. Tell him your good news. Be honest about everything bad that's happening – that's the only way he can make a valid decision.'

ASSESS FIVE

- Not every business needs to raise money at first
- Be clear about how long you will need the money for and what security you can give potential backers
- Use financial forecasts to check your business is viable and to raise sufficient amounts of money
- Take time over forecasting and err on the side of pessimism when estimating costs and turnover
- Check out regionally available funding and resources
- Decide whether you will trade before you raise money
- Know your plan inside out; practise your pitch and be clear about the message you want to convey

- Find out before a presentation who makes decisions
- Be prepared for investors to ask for more in-depth research
- Ask for the right amount first time round
- Don't be put off by negative reactions and don't exaggerate projections – try to convey competency to investors

Quick list: In fewer than ten words, list

- Whether you will self-fund the business at first and how much you will invest personally
- Which family or friends will invest or lend you money
- How much security you have for a bank loan
- Whether you are eligible for a loan guarantee
- Whether you are eligible for grants or regional resources
- Whether you need significant funds for fast growth
- What proportion of the business you plan to own (short-medium-long term)
- Possible queries about your plan from investors

Chapter Six

Starting up – how do people choose premises, buy equipment, find suppliers, develop a product, select a name, build a brand, attract customers and control cash?

Premises

Working from home is an obvious way for a start-up to cut costs. **Robyn Jones** used her spare bedroom as an office for her first five years in business. 'There were two options,' she recalls. 'One was to rent an expensive office, get a nice company car, and take on a salesperson and secretary. The other route was via my own back bedroom. I was very strict with myself. I wanted to make sure that, if I was working from home, I was working at least nine to five. Just walking down the corridor to the back bedroom where I was working from was helpful. When I was doing days of telesales on my own, I said to myself, "You can't have a coffee till you speak to a client" or "You can't have lunch till you get an appointment." The joke was that I got very hungry and very thin.'

Arthur and **Irene Allen** set up their first office at home in rural Norfolk after they won a contract to make tiny magnetic pieces for a board game. 'We subcontracted as much work as possible and took on just the straightforward assembly, which didn't require any machinery. We worked from our dining room, made a desk from a door off an old wardrobe, and propped my BBC Micro computer on it,' says Arthur. As the company grew, they expanded into the local chapel, the village hall and some old laboratories on a nearby farm.

John Frieda started a production line from the basement of his hairdressing salon, but says he realised he needed new premises when it became a logistical nightmare. 'I started selling products in forty Boots stores and within six months my products were in a thousand stores. Then I got an order for 1.2 million bottles of thickening lotion – it was like having a hit record.'

Barrie Pearson got away without having an office at first because he was always ready to visit prospective clients, or hire a hotel room to hold client meetings, but he says it became increasingly difficult. 'Getting an office in London at that time would have involved a lengthy lease, so my auditors rented me space in their offices, but it looked transient to clients and potential staff. Over the years we found better-quality accommodation, but there was never a feeling of substance. Our clients told us our offices let us down, and eventually we decided to take on premises that would allow us to double our head count. We also decided that we would be prepared to pay top-of-the-market rent for the right location, and invest thousands to kit out the offices.'

> **20/20** . . . 'When you start a business, the most important thing is survival.'
> – Richard Thwaite

It can feel like a big step to take on an office but a start-up may need to convey an impression of solidity to establish credibility. Appearance, location, convenience, size and cost are all factors in choosing a place. Sometimes the best solution is to start with a temporary arrangement.

William Sieghart was lent office space, a trestle table and phone line to set up a publishing company and, in return, agreed to work for his friend's company in Soho one day a week. 'It's a good thing to advise people to do – to set up as cheaply as possible, especially if you can get incubated and someone will provide professional services for you,' says his partner **Neil Mendoza**. 'It's important not to have to give away chunks of your company early on. I'm always advising people not to raise money but to try to scrape by in the first year or two. So many people start businesses and expect to be earning the same money as before.'

In hindsight, **Andrew Lindsay** and **Simon Scott** say they would have looked for a more cheerful office space. 'We [were] in a serviced basement office, probably the most depressing place we have ever been in our lives,' says Lindsay. 'The lady next door was into feng shui and . . . said everything was wrong. Every time we pitched to a potential client, we missed the business by a hair's breadth. We had no business. The first year we made huge losses and I remember recycling old bits of paper in the photocopier to save money. After a year on our own in the basement, we moved to another location, which was cheaper and nicer, and things started to improve.'

> **20/20 . . .** 'Remember the difference between form and substance. Fancy offices are fine but rarely create value. Start-ups with plush equipment seldom make it.'
>
> – Jeremy Seigal

Charlie Muirhead's first office was in the basement of a funeral parlour. 'We used to hear the thumping of the coffins overhead. I used to lie in bed at night and think, "What have I started? Is this going to turn into anything tangible?" ' **Martin Rutty** began working from a coal cellar in New Oxford Street. 'It was grotty and damp and we'd go out and do a job and hope the phone would ring when we got back,' he remembers.

Simon and **Anne Notley** drove out into the countryside to look for rented accommodation in which to house their iron-bed manufacturing operation – and found some chicken sheds at £3,000 each. Despite being 'leaky, horrible and freezing', the Notleys say the sheds were a good deal, especially as one was thrown in rent-free for a year. Then they opened their first shop. 'Anne's parents had an old post office outside Guildford and were running a pine shop rather half-heartedly. We basically commandeered it and they ran it for us,' says Simon. 'We used to have people go to Guildford from Essex to look at the beds and realised that we had to make it easier to look [by opening more shops]. Most competitors don't have shops but we very definitely wanted to, so people could go and see our beds – we covered them up with lovely duvets and that helped us to get a good price.'

As a retailer, **Jonathan Elvidge** budgeted up to £20,000 to fit out his first shop. 'There were a lot more costs than I had anticipated,' he remembers. 'The fit ended up costing £50,000. When you rent a shop, you don't have walls and ceiling or floors, and there's no shop front or fire alarm – and you have to have that. Then you've got sprinkler systems, cabling, electricity and air conditioning.'

With hindsight, he says, he should have paid for a retail letting agent to negotiate his rent initially. 'That agent would have wanted ten per cent of the first year's rent; they'd have worked for an hour and been paid £3,500 and at that time I would have thought, "There's no way I'm paying that much." But, instead of paying £35,000 for a shop, I might have paid £20,000 or even £15,000 a year for twenty-five years. All of a sudden, in context, that's very good value. My business partner Andrew had all the experience I lacked in the area of shop letting. It was an interesting situation because he'd been working for the landlord of Princes Quay, so it was his job to accept my naïveté. When he came on board, he renegotiated the rent. By then, we knew that we were the third most popular shop, and Andy agreed to guarantee the rent.'

> **20/20** . . . 'It's useful to have expertise working for you, but we've also employed consultants who've cost a fortune and not been good value. You have to pick carefully and identify your return.'
>
> – Jonathan Elvidge

Equipment and suppliers

Early investment in the right technology took companies such as FrameStore and ATTIK into a bigger league. 'Ours was a market waiting to happen, with the vision of using computers to create magical images,' says **Sharon Reed**. 'Early on, we bought a machine . . . with technology which allowed us to manipulate images with no degradation in quality. This was an enormous bolt-on and we began to create these fantastic images.'

James Sommerville remembers being 'blown away visually' by the demonstration of a new Apple Mac computer. 'Prior to that, our industry relied on drawing boards and scalpel blades and it was all very backroom and dirty. We moved into Apple immediately and fell in love with it. We were still very small and could afford to take the risk, and it really advanced our product offering. It seemed like a lot of money – £25,000 – and [we knew it] would be a real weight across our shoulders if it didn't work. But when we saw what this was capable of doing we had to have it. What catapulted us forward was the fact that most other design agencies didn't bother with the Mac until the late eighties. By that time, everyone at our company was faster and quicker [on it]. We had thrown all our drawing boards in the skip because we found it more accurate to work on screen.

'When we first invested in equipment, we bought this huge back-end photographic printer. That probably cost us £15,000 – sixty per cent of our initial investment – and it wasn't turning out work every day because there's only a certain part in the cycle when you need to use your back-end production facilities. It was collecting dust for three weeks out of four. As we grew, we decided to focus on areas that we would be doing every day and just buy in other things. We could have spent the money a bit better. But then, I would rather have lost £15,000 than £150,000, so it was a small price to pay for a big lesson.'

> **20/20 . . .** 'If I had started up on my own, I would have been bust within a week. I would have invested in all sorts of things I didn't need.'
>
> – Howard Leigh

Arthur Allen says a previous experience of dealing with a particular supplier, and being honest about difficulties in paying the bills, helped him when he started his own business. 'When we started Listawood, I contacted the same supplier. We had no money and were pretty fragile, but he gave us ninety days' free credit. That was an enormous support and reinforced the lesson that, if you deal with people on the basis of integrity, it's better than trying to pull a fast one.'

> **20/20 . . .** 'I am a great believer in paying my suppliers on time, if not sooner. If you can get the right goods in, you can get the clients' money in quicker. Some people say you should keep creditors waiting but that's absolute nonsense. You need to nurture the relationship. Pay them quickly to make them want to do business with you. That's clever.'
>
> – Neil Franklin

Name

Most entrepreneurs spend time researching the market and making forecasts but not every entrepreneur gives the same degree of thought to finding a name for the business. **Jan Van den Berghe** says, 'I seriously don't believe it matters . . . we had several "find a new name" sessions. Any name will do as long as it's distinctive and memorable enough. Take the top ten new brands from 2000 and I'm sure there is no line [of thought] in them.'

But some company founders, such as **James Sommerville**, say it's important not to go with the first title that comes to mind. 'We were throwing around a few names and some were really cheesy. At one point we were nearly called Blob for some bizarre reason. When we started, the industry seemed to revolve around the names of partners, and that was the norm. You are almost giving yourself a life sentence – as soon as you put your name on the front door, if you are not in the office, people are wondering where you are. There was no in-depth strategy attached to our choice of name but we thought the name ATTIK could be more of a collective rather than two heroes.'

Others warn that the obvious choices are not always the best. **Nick Austin** explains, 'I have always loved the word "imagination" because I think that's the essence of what toys are about, and I definitely wanted it in the title of the company. In the first year, I was working from home and suddenly realised we needed to register the company in order to produce some packaging in Hong Kong. Thankfully, Vivid Imaginations hadn't been registered. In hindsight what we needed to do was to go around and register the name everywhere and make sure we had a clean title, but when you've only got five minutes to register it, otherwise you're going to blow yourself out of business, you're not as diligent as you ought to be. Unfortunately, in the US there's a porn site of the same name. Everywhere else we've got the name registered but the US is a huge exception. It's very frustrating – the last thing in the world we want is to be confused with that.'

Carol Dukes and **Emma Crowe** struggled to come up with a company name not already in use. 'Every time we thought of a name, it had been registered. We were literally walking along the street and my finance director said, "What about 'ThinkNatural'?" We were on our way to a meeting with a venture capital firm, so when we got there I checked on the Internet and registered it then and there,' says Dukes. 'Interestingly, when we launched in Germany, we went through a big exercise with two pan-European branding agencies to find a new name because we felt the existing name was English-sounding. It was an expensive process and took months to come up with a shortlist of names that none of us particularly liked. The agencies were going to take this list to focus groups so we said, "Add 'ThinkNatural', just to see what happens." The focus groups said they liked it as much if not more than the other names, so we stuck with that.'

For **Adam Twiss**, it was important to find a point of differentiation. 'At the time we named Zeus, a lot of companies were being called "net" this and "net" that. Obviously if we chose something like that we'd be bland and anonymous and we decided we wanted something that didn't have "net" in its name, something short and strong and recognisable, something people could spell, hopefully, rather than a made-up name that they struggled with. We've found that people rarely forget our name and that helps us to create an identity.'

20/20 . . . 'Business is all about luck and timing, but you only have luck and timing if you are continually looking out for things that you can lock into. I bought the domain name Shave.com in 1995 for $35. We had an Internet account, but it was an address with letters and numbers rather than a name. Herbie [Dayal] and I were sitting there having a drink and one of us said, "Do you think 'Shave' has gone?" We rang up and it hadn't, so we bought the name.'

— Will King

Anna Russell and **Rob Lewis** bought their website's domain name from its US owner just at the right time. 'This guy's computer services business had just gone bust, so he was more than amenable to selling Silicon.com,' says Russell. 'We were, like, "How much do you want for it?" His outstanding debts were $25,000, so we did a deal with him and he was a happy man and we were pretty happy. A week later, we got a phone call from the same guy, who was now very pissed off because he had just had an offer for about $1 million.'

Brand message

Small businesses should beware of spending a lot of money on advertising, says one entrepreneur. 'One of our competitors went bust after spending £4 million on a television campaign and not being able to deal with the capacity of people who came in,' he says.

A brand is built through every form of communication, says **Anna Russell**. 'Branding is a lot more than just paying a public relations company. It's about how you respond when you pick up a telephone and talk to a customer, all kinds of things. You need to have an integrated approach,' she says. A company also needs to monitor how the market perceives its brand. 'We do that by having people at the front line every single day who are providing feedback and ideas, whom we're listening to. We do a lot of external research, always going back to the user and testing out their product perceptions on various different levels.'

> 20/20 . . . 'Equip yourself with an industrial-sized bullshit detector. And never ever buy any advertising in a yearbook – ninety-nine per cent of them are sold by sharks to naïve and vulnerable businesses.'
>
> – Jan Hruska

One of the simplest ways to publicise a product is to talk to key people about it. 'We educated the market through our sales force,' says Russell. 'There are major IT companies who still don't advertise online, so for us it's really about getting in front of people and talking – as simple as that. This is an area where nothing replaces just talking to people about what we do.' **Will King** also speaks of spending his first hour every morning responding to e-mails and still invests heavily in sending out free samples to win customers. 'I like enthusing people who say, "We don't know who you are." '

Simon Notley learned the value of professionalism from his experiences trying to sell futon beds. 'I began to do mail order . . . I designed this leaflet, sent off loads in the mail, and got just one sale.' When he and his wife Anne launched the Iron Bed Company, they did things a little differently. 'We knew we had to get a decent brochure so we hired an expensive photographer and studio, and ploughed the rest of our money into getting it done. That paid off because we got into all the magazines, exhibited at the Country Living fair, and that's really how we started to sell our beds.'

Shawn Taylor chose to invest in having a professional racing image designed shortly after opening his service centre. 'The image I have got is for the future. I didn't want to create an image that I had to change. It means that people think I am a bit more specialised – someone came in and thought we were a national company – but you have to sacrifice a bit in the first years until your name gets about.'

20/20 . . . 'Our marketing efforts and expenditure have been trivial: we have nice brochures and chocolate bars in reception, and try to treat people well, and that's about it.'

– Jon Moulton

Another way to publicise a product is to get the right people talking about it. Celebrity friends of **Dan Morrell** and **Sue Welland**, such as Damien Hirst, helped to promote their message about trees. 'Our first challenge was to get anyone to take us seriously, and to that end we got a lot of the cool opinion formers on our side,' says Morrell. Welland adds, 'For us, having celebrity endorsement was vital because what we are selling – carbon offset – is a dry subject. The media weren't understanding it five years ago, so one of the ways of providing the photography and news they needed was through celebrities. We tried to make the idea promotable by organisations. If you give them a payback they will be more interested in what you have to offer. Also, we wanted to separate ourselves from other green organisations and have a brand which was distinct.'

The **Finn** brothers decided that they needed to target specific users in order to generate recommendations and endorsement. 'In the mid-nineties we could see there was going to be this big American market for Sibelius, so we opened a small office in Hollywood and approached American composers to get our name around,' says **Jonathan Finn**. 'That paid off because one of the biggest names in the business bought our software, the film composer Lalo Schifrin.'

It's useful to keep a message about a complex product simple. **Charlie Muirhead** learned to describe Orchestream's business as the pithy 'air-traffic control for the Internet'. Equally, potential customers will not be slow to see through a false claim. **Richard Reed** says his vision of an unadulterated fruit drink 'informs everything from our stationery paper to what we put in our bottles. When we started, people were saying to us, "You'll get to market a lot quicker and cheaper if you just put in this and take out this." When we spoke to manufacturers they said, "Use a concentrated juice – it's a third of the price and you get a better shelf life." They were saying to us, "You don't understand" and we were, like, "No, *you* don't understand." If we'd followed their advice we would have had a rubbish company.'

> **20/20 . . .** 'To get to the luxury of doing what you enjoy takes an awful lot of hard work.'
>
> – Neil Franklin

A start-up may not have the funds to compete with the giants for advertising space but word-of-mouth recommendation is sometimes more powerful, says **Andrew Pollock**. 'Our view was that, if you do good-quality work, those clients will tell other people. We always preferred to do our marketing by working for people.'

Customer relationships

There are many reasons why people will buy a particular product: price, convenience and functionality, for example. **Nick Austin** began to glimpse another reason as a child, when he made money by going carol-singing. 'In the old days, you sold to people by having a unique selling proposition, something that differentiated you from other people,' he says. 'These days it's very difficult to differentiate your products and sustain that differentiation on pure functionality. A lot of products are sold on emotional selling propositions – the emotion of an experience.'

It's common for first-time entrepreneurs to be so intent on creating the product of their dreams that they strive to fulfil an ideal rather than an actual customer need. Be obsessed about customers, says **Charlie Muirhead**.

'This was one of the biggest lessons I learned doing Orchestream. I didn't have any experience in the industry and came up with a picture of what I thought the opportunity was. It was actually pretty close but, because it wasn't based on my experiences in front of customers, it was missing a bunch of detail which was much more important. We ended up building something to solve a problem that I was articulating, rather than our customers. It turned out we were right that it was a problem, but it meant we were very focused on building towards a vision rather than building towards a customer need. We were not obsessed about customers until Ashley Ward [now chief executive] came on board. All you have to do is solve the customer problem and then move on to the next one and the next one. It's easy to assume that new entrepreneurs are going to focus on the customer, but that's not always the case.'

> **20/20 . . .** 'Starting an agency is not complicated: it's an easy business. It's *getting* the business that's difficult, making a hundred calls to get one piece of business. I don't think we've always had good luck. It's always been graft. If you're out there making twenty calls, that generates luck – and you'll get the extra call that brings in business. But if you're not out there doing something, nothing will happen.'
>
> – Neil Mendoza

> **20/20 . . .** 'Until something has no chance of happening you have to pursue it.'
>
> – Nick Rose

It's important to be persistent, even pushy, in winning custom. **Richard Allen-Turner** of Avalon remembers the early years of attracting clients at the Edinburgh Festival. 'We'd go to the places where the acts were hanging out, get to bed in the early hours, and start again at 9.30 a.m.,' he says. His partner **Jon Thoday** says, 'Richard and I had enthusiasm and our clients could see that we were willing to work really hard for them. When we became successful at Edinburgh everyone thought we were a big organisation because we had proved we could take people from being completely unknown to being successful.'

> **20/20 . . .** 'If you're going to work for talent, you have to be on the side of that talent. If you become too friendly, you make soft deals.'
>
> – Jon Thoday

Simon Tindall remembers how Haymarket's 'revolutionary' phone sales techniques helped it to get a foothold in the publishing market. 'Space-selling of the fifties was about going out and making four to five visits per day. We realised that, if you were to telephone all day, you could make about thirty contacts and, if you got ten per cent, you had three customers. If you got a twenty-five per cent success rate with four or five, you'd have only one customer.'

John Mortimer describes how persistence combined with astuteness wins business. 'There are people who say they would start their own business if they had the opportunity – frankly, most people wouldn't know an opportunity if it hit them on the head. What you have to do is open yourself up for opportunities. As a very simple example, we got a big client in the seventies because we were up at the office at nine o'clock instead of nine thirty. The client put in a call to his regular agency and didn't get a response. He then called us saying, "I'm fed up of not getting a response at 9.30 a.m."'

20/20 . . . 'You open your doors, you put the best product out there and you give the best customer service. You just work at it, and that's really the thing.'

– Mark Constantine

Entrepreneurs also need to be persuasive in selling a product to people who don't know they want it yet, as **Alex van Someren** did. 'We've had to make our own market in encryption. We had to go out and persuade customers that there was a problem there. We found a few companies that knew about the problem but there were thousands more that we had to persuade. We hired a sales force in the US, based on one guy in the security industry who knew all the right people, and who marched around and built the business from zero to $20 million.'

Good response times, reliability, discount and 'club' offers and continuing innovation can all contribute to building loyalty in customers. Be proactive in keeping customers, says **Jan Van den Berghe**. 'Service is very important. You don't want to lose a customer, and if you lose him you want to at least know why. We had lots of angry phone calls but at least we knew what the problem was and could do something about it.'

> **20/20** . . . 'Our success has come from delivering what and when we say we're going to deliver, and invoicing what and when we say we'll invoice. Being reliable, in other words – a really basic principle. But it seems there are so many people around that can't deliver.'
>
> – Simon Needham

Be cautious about assuming ownership of a customer's goodwill. **Richard Farleigh** describes how his instincts about members developed over time. 'Often I've had entirely the wrong instincts about how to run a private members' club like Home House. I said at the start, "Maybe we could put up a board with members' photos on it." Brian [Clivaz] said to me, "That would be the daftest thing we could do."'

Cash flow

The long-term aim for any business is to make profits that can be reinvested into developing the business, its products and markets. To survive in the short term, any business has to build sales to the point at which they cover overheads – break-even, in other words. **Andrew Pollock** points out, 'When you don't have the luxury of a big firm behind you, every month you have to do enough business to cover overheads and turn it into cash as fast as you can. As a small firm, you can't take a long-term view that a big firm can take.'

Cash flow for a start-up may be lumpy and seasonal, as for **Jeremy Seigal** and **Philip Newton** when they started The Perfume Shop. 'It was a hairy old ride for a couple of years, having to pay for stock as we purchased it, and having such a heavy weighting towards Christmas. Our cash flow in October and November was a source of pain and discomfort,' they say. 'Imagine walking through a packed warehouse early in November, praying that you've bought the right stock that your customers want to buy, otherwise you wouldn't pay down the overdraft.'

Neil Franklin employed a factoring agent when he started up his company, a method that enabled him to concentrate on core activities and eliminate cash-flow headaches: the agent paid the contractor, invoiced the client and took its own cut before paying Franklin. 'It's safer that way because everyone gets paid. I like outsourcing – it makes so much sense and you can concentrate on your core activities and get rid of non-core things,' he says. 'The only reason I stopped outsourcing that function was because we grew too big.'

However, **James Keay** says it would have been a mistake for him to factor. 'Cash flow was a problem at the start. We got within twenty-four hours of factoring our invoices but we found that each month we managed to see the cash flow through. It would have been fatal for us to factor – you lose control when you have someone else chasing your customers and they're not usually as flexible as you are. It was a tricky six months at first. Obviously I put as much pressure as I could on my own customers but we were a new company and had no credit rating – and people wanted money up front.'

> **20/20 . . .** 'It's essential not to underestimate the importance of cash flow when starting out.'
>
> – Mike Altendorf

Businesses that have raised large sums of money from investors may think they're safe – in fact, they need to be extra-vigilant. **Stewart Dodd** warns, 'Never underestimate the need for cash. The temptation for many new businesses once they have raised their first round of funding is to breathe a huge sigh of relief and believe that they can go mad. But once you've raised that money you should conserve it as obsessively in the first six months as you did in the run-up. It doesn't matter how much money you have in the bank, you have to be able to justify every bit of spending. Having said that, remember that as a start-up you are in the business of creating value. Anybody can cut costs to the bone, and the result will be a healthy bank balance but a stagnant business and ultimately a slow death.'

It's useful to get into the habit of frequently comparing performance with budget. **Neil Franklin** explains, 'If something goes wrong and you have a system, you can go back and analyse the parts. You would be surprised how many businesses don't do that. People say to me, "Why are you going through the cheque stubs? You're the chief executive – you shouldn't do this." But I want to know.'

On a week-to-week basis, says **Simon Notley**, accounts must be up to date. 'You've got to have the right people helping you. It's no good employing one man and his dog. You might not want to go to one of the Big Five straightaway but you need to have an accountant that you [almost] can't afford, someone who's really good. Make sure that you have completely up-to-date and correct information.'

> **20/20** . . . 'Starting a business is traumatic. It's never easy. You are bound to have some cash-flow crises.'
>
> – William Sargent

Barry Bester says that at Topps Tiles, staff report profits from each store every Wednesday and Saturday night. 'I have always wanted to know what we were taking. If you know what you're taking on a Wednesday, if it's good you can get on the phone and encourage people; if it's bad, you can gee them up. You have to keep your eye on detail and not get carried away.' Detail counts in many ways: **Arthur and Irene Allen** got into a new market through their cost-consciousness, realising that by changing measurements they could cut nine mouse mats from a sheet, rather than the standard eight.

For **Karen Haddon**, times of trouble reinforced the need to control cash. 'What we learned from our consolidation exercise was that there was an awful lot of waste in the company. When things are going well, you let people get away with things, without restrictions. Now, even though our company is strong, we count every penny. People have to justify what they spend, and we have budgets for costs and stay within them. Things can always go wrong again.'

> **20/20** . . . 'We got over that first difficult hump within eighteen months but it was three years before we started to make a decent amount of money.'
>
> – Anne Notley

John Mortimer says that control of costs bears directly on how fast a business will grow. 'You should be looking to drive down the cost per head rather then allowing it to increase. Sometimes you just have to simply refuse to pay the prices people ask for or accept the increases that they put in for. However, you can't just cut costs: you have to ensure that your growing company is getting what it needs from its suppliers. Sometimes you have to be very creative for them.'

QUESTIONS FROM THE EDGE

Should I get to grips with every little job myself?

Andy Hobsbawm: 'Everyone has a finite amount of energy and talent and should use it on the things they are best at. Make what you've got go as far as possible. Expending energy on things you're less naturally suited to drains you faster and is a less productive use of your time.'

Carol Dukes: 'When you are literally starting up, you start small and you don't need to be fancy. You need lots of common sense and "getting on with it". The tangible things are quite easy but get harder as you get bigger and that's when you start to need people who are specialists in things that are more complex – for us, six months after launch.'

What have been your experiences in choosing a location?

Carol Dukes: 'Being outside London but not far enough outside was a drawback for us. We're close enough to have to compete with London but don't have the geographical advantage and the potential labour pool. We were also trying to recruit when everyone else was in a rush to recruit.'

Simon Needham: 'The key benefit of being designers who came from the north of England was that we had to give another ten or twenty per cent because we were not in London. If you say you're from London, people conclude. "You must be good." If you say you're from Huddersfield, it's the opposite. You have to be twenty per cent better to be equal, and that without doubt contributes to our success.'

Jan van den Berghe: 'We never saw location as a constraint. When we thought we had to be central, we moved to London. Now that that's no longer really necessary, we've moved out of London. Nothing hard or tough about it – just decide and do it. There are of course some casualties along the way – not everyone can join – but they should offset against the advantages, otherwise you've made the wrong decision.'

Barry Bester: 'You might think you want your shop to be next to Marks & Spencer but that might be the worst place you can be. For us, it's a different type of retail. People who might pop into Marks & Spencer for a sandwich are often out for the day with their families. In our business it's a thought-out purchase and people will go to a particular place for tiles'.

What's the value of a snappy slogan?

Anna Russell: 'What is essential is to be able to describe quickly what your business is about and does. The most common mistake is to think that you can have a strapline or a slogan and that's your brand and off you go, and not actually think about investing in your brand at all levels. A lot of companies think they can just announce a product and, hey, that's a bit of branding done. It's not: it's an ongoing, constant exercise which you need to live and breathe, and which everyone in your company needs to live and breathe and understand.'

How can I generate positive publicity?

Robin Hutson: 'A lot of people say to us, "You've had some fantastic press, how do you do it?" I don't think there's really a trick, other than generally trying to respect the wishes and needs of a journalist or a magazine and trying to fulfil those. There's nothing worse than a magazine needing some information and having to call three times to get it. If you respond professionally and accurately, you're far more likely to get included. It's really just about interacting and treating people with respect. You've also got to deliver – you can't just rely on publicity; and, if you hype your company a lot and there's no substance, it's suicidal.'

Simon Notley: 'We provide loan beds all the time for people to use in photo-shoots and that's far more cost-effective than spending a lot of money on advertising. We haven't done any crazy stunts. It's making sure that you keep the magazines happy so therefore you are continually feeding them stuff. Even though they phone up at the last minute, you make damn sure you have a good reputation for being able to solve their problems so that they'll come back.'

Liz Meston: 'You have to use every opportunity that's offered. I was on the radio the other day – just for half an hour – and I could have said no but I had to do it.'

What's your advice on working with customers?

Neil Franklin: 'The important thing is flexibility: being able to do what's required even when you can't do it. I go to my clients and they might say, "I like what you've done, but can you do this?" It's my job to find a way. It's all about them. I learned this from a cousin who was talking about a new man in her life. I said to her, "Why this one?" She replied, "Because he took an interest in me." It's the same with customers: they like people who have an interest in them; it gives them more confidence and you start to build trust and that's what business is all about. Don't try to please your customers: try to blow them away. You may not be indispensable, but you can get very close to that.'

ASSESS SIX

- Consider working from home or borrowing office space
- Think about communication and access arrangements for employees, suppliers and customers
- Keep costs low but don't cut corners on offices or IT
- Make your surroundings cheerful to keep up your spirits
- Build trust with suppliers
- Don't choose a name in haste
- Avoid a name that is complicated or hard to memorise
- Invest in creating a quality image
- With a complex product, keep the message simple
- Don't neglect your brand image as the company grows
- Don't assume that you own a customer's goodwill

Quick list: In fewer than ten words, describe

- Factors that affect where you start up
- The kind and price of equipment you will need initially
- Whether you will buy, lease, hire or borrow equipment
- Additional training you need
- Where and when to seek it

- Who are potential suppliers and resellers
- Your sales dialogue to potential customers
- Methods by which you will control cash initially
- Qualities you want to convey in your name and brand
- What you want customers to say about your business
- How will you build loyalty to your product or service

PART THREE

GETTING THE SHOW ON THE ROAD

Chapter Seven

In the early years of starting up, how do entrepreneurs cope personally and practically, handle new responsibilities and establish credibility? How do they handle a crisis?

Practical issues

For the first months, an entrepreneur is often working alone. 'You have a dream plan but what you don't realise is that, when you're in a small office by yourself, it's not the same as in a big company,' says one entrepreneur. 'If your computer takes a nosedive and it takes five hours to sort out, during that time nobody's doing any work.' Most new start-ups, says **Heather Rabbatts**, 'particularly when they have huge aspirations and their people have come out of big corporate structures, miss the infrastructure support.'

It's important to be committed to finishing tasks, says **Richard Thwaite**. 'It's fine to start small [but] companies need to make sure that anything they do gets done quickly and as well as it can possibly be done.'

> **20/20** . . . 'Ask yourself: do I really want to be the person who goes home at night with everything resting on my shoulders? Do I want to be the person that keeps the energy going when times are tough? Or do I want to be led by someone like that?'
> – Charlie Muirhead

Gerard Basset and **Robin Hutson** kept their day jobs until just a month before they opened the doors of their first hotel. 'The hardest thing was that we were doing all the work ourselves,' says Basset, who says he learned to be versatile. 'We had no night porter, no maintenance staff, and Robin's dad used to come at weekends to do repairs. The guests would say, "The loo doesn't work – what do I do?" and I didn't know. It was tiring.'

Liz Meston's biggest worry was about getting customers. 'I used to worry all the time when we were smaller. We had thirty customers in Suffolk and I would think, "Are we going to have any more, ever? Is anyone else going to come? Where will they come from?" ' For **Simon Needham**, bad spelling caused problems. 'By making mistakes, we learned quickly not to make them again. Our spelling was so bad that we decided it would be more cost-effective to pay someone to proofread all our copy, rather than to reprint everything. It's entertaining to think about it now, but distressing at the time.'

> **20/20** . . . 'There's a big difference between fear and concern. Concern motivates me – fear doesn't.'
>
> – Neil Franklin

Richard Reed learned a great deal in a short time. 'For four years I was in a professional environment learning so many different skills, yet when you set up on your own you find yourself making ridiculous mistakes – really simple things. For instance, before you order fifty fridges, why don't you just order one and make sure you're happy? But it's Monday morning and there's this salesman saying, "Come on, you've got to order it at this moment to get the best deal." The fact you're trying to think of everything means you'll probably make those mistakes. It's about time management and being smart, rather than working every hour that God sends. Often, you get caught in the heat of the moment. You have to stand back and say, "Is this right?" Literally, go out and sit in the toilet for ten minutes.'

> **20/20** . . . 'We still get stressed over the same things as we did fifteen years ago but it's like having a kid: the first time he takes a fall, you panic; when he's four and comes running with a cut knee, it's like, "Oh dear me." '
>
> – Simon Needham

Personal issues

Business activities can be incredibly intense and time-consuming, as **Roger Myers** points out. 'If you want to get involved with the restaurant business, you have to realise that you're going to be there, and you'll want to be there, all the time. If it's successful you never want to go home. You want to do it again, because it's fun. Of course, if it's not a success, you don't want to go near it.'

Because of this, it's important to try to enlist support on a personal level, says **William Sargent**. 'Before you found the business, you need your [domestic] partner on board. By definition a new business is undercapitalised. The last thing you need if you're struggling with the bank manager is for your domestic partner to say, "I'm fed up with this."'

> **20/20** . . . 'Our expectations were completely different to the reality – we had been partners in a big firm advising small and medium-sized companies and we thought we understood small businesses.'
>
> – Andrew Pollock

Not everyone naturally springs out of bed at six every morning, but many entrepreneurs say they notice themselves becoming highly energised during the start-up period. The flip side is burnout. **Maziar Darvish** closely associates the speedy growth of his Internet Business Group with the fact that 'I haven't had a proper holiday for nearly five years.' Meanwhile, **Nick Rose** juggled studying for his university exams with building his revision venture Revise.it, commuting between London and Oxford by coach in the early hours of the morning and working up to sixty hours at a time.

'I took a week off, went to Jamaica and really switched off,' he remembers. 'I came back to Oxford, went to bed feeling jetlagged, woke up and couldn't move for the next week. The doctors thought I had a virus, but . . . when your body is so used to working and then switches off, it takes a while to recover. My mum came down to Oxford and took me home. Running a business is all about the highs and lows and unfortunately, if you get so much out of those highs, the lows hit pretty hard. You have to work all hours and the upside is worth it, but you have to see the symptoms of stress.'

Jonathan Elvidge also reports feeling the strain physically. 'In the early years, I was constantly feeling nauseous for about a year, and the doctor couldn't find anything the matter. I was sick every day. Finally, I concluded it had been stress. It happened when everything was still very difficult. It helped me to realise that nothing is important when you compare it to having your health. I would rather be selling the *Big Issue* on the street every day and be well, and, once it comes down to that, nothing else is a problem. That puts things into perspective and, once you come to terms with it, you tend to stop worrying.'

Charlotte Barker speaks of keeping a balance. 'When I came back from trade shows there was always a bit of an anticlimax. I was so buzzed up from performing in front of people, and when I came back it was hard going. You have to get the balance of working hard and playing hard. I've not had a social life for years, or a holiday for four years. That's the sacrifice. But you also have to say to yourself that it's OK to take a holiday. It's OK to finish on a Friday afternoon a bit early.'

Uncertainty about the future also causes strain. **James Millar** explains, 'When it's good, it's very good, but it can change to being tough. And when it's tough you get used to it being tough, and suddenly it becomes good again. That swing and change can be emotionally draining. We were voted the best home-shopping grocery company in the world by a survey on the Internet. The same day, we got our accounts, which said that we'd made a loss of £60,000. And I thought to myself. "How do we deal with both of these things? Which news do we tell our staff?" '

> **20/20** . . . 'We try to have a balance between making sure everyone has got a pay cheque and keeping the banks happy. It's not only about making money, because if it was we would be out there doing dog food commercials and our bank manager would be really pleased.'
>
> – James Sommerville

For any entrepreneur, active responsibility goes with the territory, says **Nicola Murphy**. 'Even now, if I'm on holiday and haven't had a couple of calls from the office, I don't like it. I worry if I don't know what's going on. I walk through the building and see all these people whose mortgages depend on me. It's a big responsibility. I still feel guilty if I've got a dentist's appointment and I'm going to be late.'

Mark Smith and **Tim Connolly** describe how they hired a personal coach to dispel some of the tension of running a business. 'One of the big things I've learned . . . has been how to live with constructive tension, and accept that not everyone's going to agree with what I'm doing all the time,' says Connolly. 'It's a big thing to come to terms with, the fact that you are not going to get a hundred per cent mandate. The easy way out is to restrict yourself to the lowest common denominator of what everyone accepts.'

Andrew Lindsay remembers the contrast represented by The Union's first Christmas party during one depressing start-up patch. 'At the party held by the company we'd come from, there would be vintage champagne and the prizes in the raffle would be trips to New York. For our first party at the Union we were at the pub eating sausages and mash, wearing limp party hats, unable even to summon the energy to pull the crackers.'

However, **Andrew Pollock** recalls an early Christmas party as a more joyful occasion. 'The year had been difficult; it could have gone either way. At our party, I was watching everyone enjoying themselves and suddenly thought, "We've got good people. We're developing good clients. We can't lose."'

> **20/20** . . . 'To survive you need lots of options. It's risky when things don't work out but most of it is down to the bounce time – how quickly can you bounce back?'
> – Mark Constantine

Credibility

In the early days one of the most arduous tasks is to establish credibility with customers and suppliers, says **Charlotte Barker**. 'People generally won't listen and won't take time to listen. If I was talking to a store, they would say, "We don't deal with board games." I might try to say, "This is more than a board game." But people would cut me off before they heard what it was about. That can be discouraging when you're on your own.'

Jeremy Seigal was 'thrown off more stands at perfume trade shows than I care to remember' when starting The Perfume Shop. 'It just encourages you to try, try and try again that much harder. It was essential to establish sufficient critical mass in the number of stores, so that we had a chance to be taken seriously by manufacturers.'

The early challenge was for the shop to get supplies from the major fragrance houses. 'The industry itself did not welcome a new entrant,' explains **Philip Newton**, 'and preferred to retain distribution through existing traditional channels. That may have remained the case for longer had it not been for the Monopolies and Mergers inquiry into the selective distribution of the major houses. Jeremy and I gave evidence to this and . . . it was quite clear that things would change. Chanel was the first to want to talk to us, and from then on, over a period of five years, the majority of the remaining houses offered us direct supply. The key to our success was continually knocking on doors. It's not being knocked down that matters, it's getting up.'

> **20/20 . . .** 'Anyone who says they are not lucky, when they have a success, should be looked at with some degree of circumspection. Luck has played an important part for The Perfume Shop – right time, right place, right offer, right people.'
> – Philip Newton

Brian Clivaz says the initial difficulty was to get people to believe in the vision he had for a club. 'The building, although magnificent, was seen by many at that time to be in the wrong location. I felt that the location was perfect and this proved to be the case. The biggest challenge was to keep the confidence of the investors and the bank during the development phase, when substantial sums of money were being spent for no apparent return. The strain of running a company which had no income and a high burn rate is not to be recommended. Moving from the building phase into the operating phase was [also] a difficult period, especially as we had demand from members to use the club while the builders were still finishing their work.'

It took **David Landau** three years to establish an operation that made a profit. 'It was just a question of when the company would be cash-positive in day-to-day trading. It was difficult to convince our distributors to go on, but I was sure it was going to work and be successful, and that gave us strength to continue. Every week we were selling more copies and getting more ads.'

The main obstacle was that nobody believed in the *Loot* concept at first. 'People wouldn't believe us when we said the adverts were free. We thought we would be flooded by calls but the phone was dead. There was this feeling of "nothing comes free in life" – people were saying, "Send me the bill." The only way of getting that message across would have been to spend vast amounts on marketing but I'm not sure that would have been productive. Our approach was simply to let word of mouth take its course, with people telling each other, "I put my car in and sold it and never paid a penny." '

Dan Morrell and **Sue Welland** say one of their difficulties was that people didn't understand their message about carbon offset. Future Forests was 'pigeonholed into environmental budgets, which tended to be small' and Welland adds, 'People might have heard of Woodland Trust or recycled paper . . . the most difficult thing was to explain the idea of Future Forests in a cold call.'

Another problem can be the lack of a track record. The big difficulty for **Robyn Jones** was that every prospective client wanted to see a contract in operation, and at first she had none. 'It was easy to talk confidently on the phone and use the word "we", and I felt confident in that I knew I could fulfil their requirements because I was seeing what they had already got. But when they asked, "Can I come and see some business?" I was stumped. I had no business. That was the hardest part because at first, I couldn't offer that.'

> **20/20** . . . 'Our business has sometimes been so hard that, if we didn't believe in it and see that the goal was worth going for, we'd have been foolish to continue.'
>
> – Moya Crawford

Nick Austin says he found it difficult to get people to take him seriously. 'We wanted to pick up the rights to a television show called *Captain Scarlet* and I knew the company that owned the rights. I suddenly realised the difference between being "Nick Austin, managing director of Matchbox" and "Nick Austin, entrepreneur". People said, "We enjoyed working with you at Matchbox and we have no doubt you can do it, but we can't risk giving our property to you because you're a start-up."

'When we went to see people, we presented our financial credentials as soon as we could, but it wasn't a big enough amount of money to turn people's heads. We had to convince people we were a serious operation . . . that our plan would work.

'I remember my first presentation to Woolworth's,' he adds. 'They said, "Well, Nick, you do realise that new suppliers have to transact over £1 million of business in their first year – otherwise it's not worth it.' I thought, "Holy mackerel!" You just don't think about that when you're in a big business but it frightened the living daylights out of me. I feel sad for entrepreneurs who are faced with big company bureaucracy – the odds are stacked against [them] because big companies find it inconvenient to have to trade with small companies.'

Kevin Bulmer says it's important to get the timing right when launching a product. 'We started talking to people a little bit too early. It often takes years to get things in place for a property, and we weren't ready to do a deal, but we wanted people to know we were developing Astro Knights. We started to go to television festivals; we would make selective appointments to corral the opinions of broadcasters, production companies and licensing agents, just to get a feel for what was happening. A couple of people whose opinions we tried to secure early as a guiding light said when we approached them again, "Why are you still talking to us about this?" Maybe they thought we were ready to do a deal when we were first talking to them, when in fact all we had was documents and sketches. We were looking for advice and they probably thought we were looking to do a sales pitch.'

What stung most for **Simon Rees** was not picking up business, not for any good reason. 'We would talk to people who would say, "We think you're the best and the service you provide would be brilliant and the price is fine, but the board has decided they'd like a Big Five auditor." That was really frustrating.'

He and **Andrew Pollock** continued to talk to existing contacts, and eventually broke through. 'I think it takes about seven years to get a reputation established in our sector,' says Pollock. 'Turning forty [myself] after six years in business also helped. In your thirties you spend your time selling to people in their forties and fifties – but, once you join them, people find it easier to buy from you. It's a conservative business: people don't change their accountants overnight, it takes a while.'

Carol Dukes found herself caught up in the dotcom hype of the late nineties. 'You had to co-operate to get the name of your company out there, but it was like being under a microscope,' she says. 'All we were doing was setting up a business, and the world's media was watching. It was a mad time, with so much analysis of a tiny sector. People who were genuinely in the business knew there were rules: find the right people, make your money last, get the business to a point where what comes in the door is bigger than what goes out.'

> **20/20** . . . 'It's much easier to get people to do business if you say, "Hello, I'm from EMAP" or "I'm from Carlton." '
> – Carol Dukes

Persistence and reliability are keys to being taken seriously, says **James Keay**. 'The way to get credibility with suppliers is by doing exactly what they ask of you – do what they want instead of saying, "Can I send it next week?" If you do that and pay upfront the first time, they begin to trust you. There were people who didn't want to give us accounts and we had to prove we were true to our word.'

At first a start-up may have to take any work it can get, but some short cuts can damage a business. **Robyn Jones** reports how 'one supplier said, "Oh, cash on delivery, it'll have to be." I thought, no. That's very Mickey Mouse. I thought, "I want an account." You have this unseen authority when you're part of a conglomerate, but instead of saying yes to this supplier, I didn't work with them.' **David Abraham** was also prepared to say no 'to clients that quite honestly had a short-termist view of advertising. It's less difficult when the economy is bubbling along quite nicely . . . By concentrating on quality and value, we found ourselves becoming profitable.'

Another way to win credibility is to make good calls, as **Adam Twiss** describes. 'When we started in 1995, it was very difficult to predict exactly where the Internet was going. There's always an issue with emergent technologies because a whole lot of hype goes with them – and a lot of spend temporarily. As three people, without external funding, trying to compete with an organisation ten or a hundred times our size, our difficulty was to try to read the trends. We'd been on the Internet not since its academic beginning but since it started to become a glint in the eye of the mainstream, and as a result had seen things develop and had seen where things had taken off and the directions people had already gone in. As a result, we understood the market and customer drivers.'

> **20/20** . . . 'The hardest thing is when people say, "You're so successful now" and I think, "No, we've so far to go." I hate it because they think it's successful and I think, "It's bound to collapse now." '
>
> – Liz Meston

In 1997 FrameStore bought the Computer Film Company. **William Sargent** says he and **Sharon Reed** won credibility internally 'by being right and making the judgment calls. We made the call that the film industry was going to slow up by thirty per cent and it was actually sixty-five per cent. We made our redundancies in May when business was booming . . . we sat everyone down and explained that the bottom was going to fall out of the market. We made eight redundancies, a fifteen per cent cut in the company's strength. No one else made a single cut until October, when many companies had to cut by fifty per cent. The principle is that, if it's right for the business, it's right for the employees, the shareholders, the customers and the creditors. If all you do is focus on the business and put it ahead of everything else, you won't go wrong.'

Crisis

When crisis hits, it may feel like the end of the road after months of struggle. **Nick Austin** speaks of the moment when he discovered his business was headed for disaster. 'We'd been in business for less than a year and we imported ninety per cent of our products from China. It was during the first Bush era and they wanted to encourage China to join the GATT [General Agreement on Tariffs and Trade] agreement – but China was reluctant to do so. One way that the Western governments forced them to think seriously was to apply certain [import] quotas to nonstrategic industries, including toys and some textiles. In deciding quotas, the EU looked at how much business you had already done, but of course we had no track record. It was awful. I remember being in New York when I heard, and I lay back in despair on my hotel bed and thought, "Just as we thought everything was going well . . ." '

Austin and his colleagues went through the regulations and eventually found a loophole. 'If you were a new company you could have a tiny little bit of quota, and someone jokingly said, "Open a thousand companies – that'll show them." It was like, "That's it!" They couldn't stop us doing that so all of us started filling out company application forms and we formed a hundred and fifty new companies in one day. We used to laugh about the fact that we were the only company less than six months old that already had a hundred and fifty subsidiaries!

'In all of our crises, we managed to creatively think our way through. None seriously damaged or threatened our viability. The problem is that, when a crisis happens in the early years, you as an entrepreneur don't usually have expertise and resources on your doorstep. We've had a couple of nasty lawsuits from people saying, "You've infringed my patent – we want five per cent of your sales for the last five years as recompense." In those moments you think, "Oh, my God!" but it's amazing how you get out: you either negotiate your way out or creatively find a way though. An ability to problem-solve is something that entrepreneurs have to develop quickly if it doesn't come naturally. You have to find a direct solution or a lateral solution.'

20/20 . . . 'One of the first things to learn is that failure is your own fault, and not the system's. That makes failure an opportunity.'

– John Mortimer

Starting up brings little crises and big ones. **Sonita Alleyne** remembers, 'There was a point when there was only about four of us in the company and we were just coming off the back of a really big contract. We were all so busy working on that that we forgot to sell anything for the future. Suddenly, in April, we stuck our heads out and said, "Oh, God, we've got no income." I had to keep the company going on £400 a month until the next big deal came in. It was one of those moments when it was a question of, "Are we going to give up?" You must keep selling: keep the balance within the company of people that do things and people that sell things.'

FrameStore enjoyed early success but growth in profits fell at the end of the eighties, says **Sharon Reed**. 'I remember a client saying, "Everywhere I go, I hear FrameStore is the place to go." I thought that was dangerous, because ours is an industry that's terribly fashion-conscious. We were trading better than ever and people kept saying,

"The recession's coming." ' Over the next six months, business dried up and profits dropped by 90 per cent. FrameStore decided to focus its efforts, consolidate assets, pay off all the debt it could and manage its way through the recession. 'The thing that saved us was that we had spread ourselves across different markets and we had a very good relationship with the bank,' says Reed. 'We clawed our way out within about twelve months.'

> 20/20 . . . 'We never felt we were on Easy Street and were never complacent. If something can go wrong, it will, so just be prepared.'
>
> – Gail Federici

Profits at Speed Couriers were also affected by the recession, and the situation worsened when its founder **Martin Rutty** crashed his hang-glider and broke his neck, putting himself out of action for weeks. His partner **Tim Gilbert** says, 'I felt there wasn't any option but to get the business back on its feet. We were besieged by debt and Martin had moved to Shropshire and was a bit low, stuck at home. He said, "What do you want me to do?" and I said, "Most businesses in a recession go bust due to lack of cash. Get on the phone every single hour and ask for that money we're owed. And don't go near the bank manager." '

Gilbert says his biggest challenge was to keep the bank manager onside. 'One morning, I knew he was about to close us down and change the locks on the premises. There was a tense encounter, in which he reached down for his briefcase and I caught his eye and said, "I'll get it back for you." There was this long pause, then he said, "All right, then." We were that close to losing it.'

In a crisis situation, says Rutty, many people find it hard to take action, and instead let things drift and get worse. 'Doing something is absolutely essential. I like that quote from [investor and author of *The Zulu Principle*] Jim Slater: "The first cut is the cheapest." No matter how much it costs you, doing something quickly is better than letting it drift, no matter how painful it is.'

> 20/20 . . . 'I don't often see something as being a hurdle. If there's a hurdle there, you just clamber over it.'
>
> – James Keay

Listawood's turnover was increasing after three years, and so were staffing levels, but keeping pace was the company's loss. 'We doubled our overall loss to £24,000,' remembers **Arthur Allen**. 'We were surprised, as we'd been working hard. We were horrified at the dip.' **Irene Allen** remembers vividly the day she discovered the news. 'It was my fortieth birthday, the bank manager was due [to see us] in a couple of days, and my father was staying with us. We sat through a ghastly meal, unable to reveal what was going on, but fortunately my staff had organised a bouquet so when they delivered the flowers it gave me the perfect excuse to burst into tears.'

The pair went back and analysed the accounts, and discovered all the losses had taken place in the first quarter. 'It was undoubtedly very difficult, but this didn't seem quite as bad,' says Arthur Allen. 'The following year, we made healthy profits, which wiped out all our losses and increased sales dramatically. It taught us the value of management accounts.'

> **20/20** . . . 'In the early years, we were talking about survival, not growth; we were just doing what it took.'
>
> — Irene Allen

William Carey didn't anticipate that his firm's parent company would shortly sell investment trusts to other houses. 'We could no longer say we had £400 million under management, so that was a frightening moment,' he says. 'How were we going to persuade fund managers to join us when there was nothing to run? We were told we had to cut costs by thirty-five per cent and had a pretty open meeting with all the guys who had joined. We said, "We can cut staff or take a pay cut. We didn't lose anyone but people took that big cut, and I think they knuckled down. They were always convinced we could do something. The most satisfying moment was after about eighteen months, when we made more money than we spent. That relieved a lot of the pressure about one's responsibility to the people who work here.'

In the late eighties, **James Sommerville** and **Simon Needham** made redundancies as recession set in. 'We were still solely in Huddersfield and weren't generating enough business to keep us going,' says Needham. 'We were paying a lot of people wages without making money. We were demoralised and questioned during that period whether to keep going, whether it was worth it. We did speak to a lawyer and he said, "Look, why don't you give it all you've got for three months, a hundred and ten per cent, and if it hasn't happened, then do something else?" We came to the decision that we would give it one last go. Basically we did lots of new business, made call after call, and that got us back on our feet.'

Crisis has been good for ATTIK, says Sommerville – it made them analyse what they were doing. 'In an economic crisis, your phones may not ring as much, but you also wake up and think, "We've really got to tighten our belts." There's no surplus whatsoever. That could include the head count but also includes the way you operate. In good times the pace is quick and things get missed. In the tight and difficult times it's a good spring-clean period – a reality check. Externally you have no control but you have complete control over what's going on inside. It's not a nice thing to go through, but when you look back you have usually improved in some way.'

> **20/20** . . . 'Crises are, in hindsight, good for a business. That's when you really learn and grow in your management skills. Your instincts are usually right but you'll never be blind-sided by the things you worry about most.'
>
> – Jeremy Seigal

QUESTIONS FROM THE EDGE

As an entrepreneur, what have been the hardest things to handle personally?

Terry Pullen: 'Whatever the result of your labours, good or bad, you never ever feel that you totally finish the job. There's always more to do, and if you get that out of kilter it can be damaging to mind, body and soul. You need to be totally inspired to keep going against all the odds all of the time. The way to avoid that need for perfection is to ensure that you enjoy the highs – and it's important to recognise that principle not just for you, but for your team. You also need to ensure that you respond to the lows in a positive way. They are only an opportunity to get better.'

Neil Franklin: 'In my early days as an entrepreneur, we were sitting there earning X amount but spending more. That's lesson number one for an entrepreneur – don't spend all your wealth. I read a book which taught me to save ten per cent of my earnings. It was too easy to earn and spend money.'

Nigel Legge: 'When you're working for a big firm you have a nice salary, a nice bonus and life is pretty safe. Then you embark on something like this, which is in the unknown not just for you but for people that depend on you. I was lucky to have all the support I needed but it was quite stressful on occasion to wonder whether there was a chance of letting people down. One doesn't go home and say, "There's a chance this might not work." But we were awake to the possibility. You have to work out what you're going to do if it all fails – and then you have to carry on and believe in your colleagues.'

How does family life affect your life as an entrepreneur?

Nicola Murphy: 'Both Jane [Wynn] and I have got kids and it does refocus your priorities. It's made me fiercer and more decisive with regard to the business. Before, if someone buggered something up, I'd think, "Let's not give them a warning," but now I'm protective of the business's success because I think, "That's a legacy for my children." '

Nick Austin: 'Ever since being a teenager I've had a really strong, almost excessive, work ethic. Getting married and having kids was good for me – it gave me a sense of balance. I suddenly realised that being in the office at 8 p.m. every night and falling asleep in front of the nine o'clock news when I got home was a mug's game.'

James Keay: 'I don't leave the office till I know what I've got to do the next morning. If I go home having not closed down the day's work, I'm going to go home and start thinking about it. This way, I'm able to leave the office and switch off. My wife is more than happy with that. I used to have the home phone number in the adverts and the phone would go at 3 a.m. when someone took our number out of the advert in an emergency.

Then it moved to my mobile number and now it's someone else's mobile number and not out of hours. If there was an important job I might say, "Here's my number" but I don't let it rule things. You've got to set your parameters.'

How do you handle pressure?

Mark Constantine: 'You need to proceed by facing up to difficulties. Everything is down to attitude. It's boring, but what's a problem to one person is a challenge to another. Everyone is going to have things that they hate doing but you have to address them – whatever it is that winds you up.'

Adam Twiss: 'At the start, you worry about where the money's going to come from to pay for your accommodation. That's different to the pressure you're under from your board to deliver X per cent revenue this quarter compared to last quarter – it's part and parcel of being involved in a rapidly growing business. I've always been a bit of a workaholic, and can sustain that when I enjoy it and am passionate about it all. I rarely feel the need to take lots of time off.'

How important is it to stop to celebrate your successes?

Anna Russell: 'In the space of less than a year, we launched three new products as a business. It's only when you've done it that you look back and say, "Did we really do that in such a short time?" I think it's important to step back – not to be self-congratulatory but to look at why this leads you forward. We do celebrate success, but we probably don't celebrate the small successes enough. We should always be looking at ways to improve communication of the small successes. Put together, they mean a lot.'

William Sargent: 'We celebrate the achievements of the people we work with but we don't boast, nor do we expect people to highlight our failures. You need to be quiet about your successes because things go up and things go down.'

How did you increase your credibility?

Adam Twiss: 'The great thing about the early days was that we did everything over the Internet and no one knew how large we were. We sold to a lot of customers through guerrilla methods. We'd impregnate a company by selling them a very low-level product and when we wanted to sell into a larger project we could say, "We've been a good supplier for two years and this guy in your company will act as our referee." '

Aziz Cami: 'When I set up a design business for the first time, we had a small office in Covent Garden. A big potential customer wanted to come and see us, so we talked all the other companies on the other floors into pretending they were part of our business.'

Richard Thwaite: 'We put in a CD-sound-quality phone system that played music on hold – when people called us they thought they'd got through to a big company. We also took PLC status in 1992. Hardly anyone realised that, to be a PLC at that time, you only needed to have £50,000 of paid-up share capital. It meant everyone thought we were quoted.'

Andrew Hobbs: 'We've always operated as a blue-chip company. There was no way a three-branch retailer could afford to go on buying trips to New York and the Far East, but we thought, "That's how the big companies would do it" – so we did it, even if it meant flying Aeroflot. The only way to become a multiple is to think like one.'

Have you ever considered walking away from your business?

Jonathan Hartnell-Beavis: 'There was no question of giving up – we had sunk a lot of our own money into the venture and I would probably have had to mortgage my bike to get out. After four years I eventually paid off the credit-card bill, which was a champagne moment. Of course, I had to pay for the champagne on my credit card, too.'

Neil Franklin: 'In martial arts they taught me that the only measurement is success. A lot of sportsmen will, say, do fifty press-ups. In martial arts, we never had a number, we just did it till we could do it no more, and then we'd add another one on. That way, we kept bettering ourselves. If you say, "I'm only going to work three hours a day" it's no good being an entrepreneur. The whole point is to stretch yourself, but not to the point where you lose your elasticity. You've got to get as near to the edge as possible.'

ASSESS SEVEN

- Be versatile – you will almost certainly need to tackle practical details during your first year of business
- It can be a false economy to do everything yourself – pay someone to do jobs that you find hard
- Sometimes it's better to stand back and think laterally
- Develop patience and a methodical approach
- Ask for backup from friends and family or consider seeing a personal coach
- Dismantle too-high expectations, including your own
- Be ready to adapt your product to the market
- In a crisis, doing something is usually better than doing nothing
- Crisis periods can refine and improve your business

Quick list: Describe times when you have

- Been realistic about what you will achieve, and when
- Tackled jobs you've never done before
- Recognised when your productivity drops
- Taken responsibility for other people's welfare
- Refused to take no for an answer
- Negotiated a way out of a tough situation

Chapter Eight

Building a workforce, managing growth and change. How do entrepreneurs know when to recruit? What sorts of people do they employ? How do they motivate, develop and retain good people? What kind of culture do they create?

Recruiting

By hiring other people, an entrepreneur creates breathing space, which may improve the company's chances of success in the long term. However, extra sales may be needed in the short term to cover the increase in overhead. In the early days recruitment can be something of a balancing act, says **James Keay**. 'I took on my first person a few months after I started. I was doing more work than I could handle, working for fifteen hours a day. As we grew, and got people going off on holiday, suddenly that extra work needed covering and it was me that stepped in. It can be difficult – you think, "Maybe I should employ more people." But at the same time you want them to be kept busy and you don't want to overstaff the office.'

> **20/20** . . . 'Creating a real business takes much longer than you first may think. It's people that matter, and putting a good team together is a lengthy process.'
>
> – Jeremy Seigal

Robyn Jones says she was slow to recruit initially because she was cautious about spending money and wanted to monitor everything herself. 'I didn't keep the momentum going, whereas if I'd had somebody selling I'd have grown more quickly. I was doing everything, from invoice clerk to health and safety. My work came in through recommendation – in the early days, a lot of word-of-mouth and from visits to potential clients. The problem was that I put all my effort into opening up business and I forgot about telesales. I'd made all these phone calls originally and all these leads came up, but when I rang back, they said, "You've missed the boat." '

How does an entrepreneur recognise the right person to hire? After the job description has been written and the characteristics of the ideal person defined, many entrepreneurs say they go by instinct. **Robin Hutson** reflects, 'I used to think that you could train anyone to do anything. I don't believe that any more. I now believe that nice people give nice service. If you start off with someone who's personable and friendly and wants to interact with people, you can train them technically. Service isn't that complicated but with some people you just bash your head against the brick wall – and, no matter what you do, you can't really train them.'

Mark Constantine believes that 'in any business under fifty people, everyone has to be multitalented'. **Heather Rabbatts** went from managing a large organisation to managing a handful of people, and observes, 'This start-up environment lends itself to people who like getting things done rather than people who just like thinking about how things *should* be done. If everyone has to carry their own weight, no one can hide. In a big organisation you can be sitting in your corner quietly getting away with things. Here, if someone doesn't deliver, it's noticeable.'

Arthur and **Irene Allen**, based in rural Norfolk, saw the potential in local workers. 'Thirteen years ago, women in the countryside were very underemployed and there was all this talent we could get hold of,' says Irene. 'We were taking our children to school at the same time, and we'd chat. These women saw I was the same as them.'

20/20 . . . 'When you come across good people . . . it's a good idea to hire them, even if you don't have a job for them.'
– Jon Thoday

Using a recruitment agency to find staff may be an unwelcome cost but **Maziar Darvish** discovered that it was a mistake to rely too heavily on his own contacts. 'We were aware of recruitment consultancies, but viewed them as hugely expensive. We were going through networks of people we knew and thought this would ensure that we would get people to fit the company's culture. [But] people who fit into a culture don't necessarily have enough experience of management to cope in a company that's growing fast. Given that most of the founders were very young, our network didn't include people with five years' experience in anything at all. The upside was that we got a lot of energy and enthusiasm – the downside was not just a limitation, but a certain amount of reinvention of the wheel.'

As a small company, it's not always easy to attract bright people, says **Barrie Pearson**. 'I passionately believe that small companies must attract, reward and retain the calibre of person who would join the most successful companies in the market sector, but recruiting my first executive proved extremely difficult. Three times in succession, I recruited an outstanding individual, they signed an acceptance letter and in the final week before their agreed joining date they telephoned me to say they had got cold feet about joining a one-man band.'

20/20 . . . 'When I was interviewing staff, I said, "I can't promise I'm going to get any more business and I can't promise you a fantastic future career." I was always very honest throughout the whole process.'

– Robyn Jones

The key is to persuade potential employees that the company is going places. 'We make people believe that they have no life if they are not doing things with us,' says one entrepreneur. 'That's pretty powerful when you're trying to get good people to work with you.' Zeus emblazoned its logo on a silver sports car to recruit around Cambridge. 'It was about giving the keys to the car to one of our employees for the weekend, who would drive off and see friends, who would think, "That's a cool company," ' says **Adam Twiss**. 'The cost of the car per year was the cost of recruiting one person through a recruitment company, so it probably paid for itself.'

> **20/20** . . . 'Hiring a person is like buying a house: you can
> never quite afford the one you want but you try your best and
> sometimes you can be lucky. The secret is to find someone
> good and then let them do the hiring.'
> — Neil Mendoza

Andy Hobsbawm describes how the dotcom peak temporarily affected employee psychology. 'Everyone thought they were entitled to get rich overnight. It's very difficult to recruit and manage people who have such ludicrous expectations. I had to sell people on why they should join our company to a degree that was almost crazy. People knew they could get ten offers just by walking out the door. It was an economy of immediate rewards and instant gratification. We had two pay reviews per year and sometimes total wage costs would inflate by as much as twenty per cent every six months. At that time, you would lose some of your best people if you didn't do that and everyone in the services business was competing largely on the strength and depth of their talent.'

Not every employee has to be full-time, and some companies run entirely on freelance capacity. Some entrepreneurs, such as **James Sommerville**, also mention the value of a nonexecutive director. 'I would definitely encourage a young business to bring in a nonexecutive finance director – I think that person becomes the backbone of the business, really. We would have introduced someone sooner if we had clocked on to the potential benefits. If that person starts to understand your business, they will give more than just financial advice – when you are making decisions, they give an objective view. If nothing else, it gets you around the table once a month to talk about things that are important.'

> **20/20** . . . 'I'm always inspired by speaking to the chairman of
> this or that company – it's inspirational to pick someone's
> brains.'
> — Simon Needham

What if a hire turns out to be a mistake? **Tim Connolly** and his partner **Mark Smith** began hiring at a faster rate when several opportunities arose at the same time, but client feedback showed them they had slipped up in some cases. 'We tried to get the right people for the right roles in some difficult jobs – and convinced ourselves that the people we recruited were up to it. The truth is, they probably weren't,' says Connolly. 'We pride ourselves on being collaborative and transferring skills [and] some people we brought on board as employees and contractors didn't understand those standards. Our clients were coming back and saying, "These don't feel like Partners for Change people," and one even said, "I know who your people are, because they ooze the values."'

> **20/20** . . . 'Take great care when recruiting – don't employ someone you have any doubts about – you're better off not having someone than having someone who turns out to be unsuitable. If you have any doubts at interview they will almost always turn out to be well founded. Take up references.'
>
> – Ben Finn

At a senior managerial level, the stakes are higher, says **Paul Varcoe**. 'You have to be absolutely sure of your hires at high levels. It's worth spending months on it because a mistake is very expensive. The only way you can avoid a mistake is to be superb at understanding what makes someone tick and get as many references as possible. There's no substitute for experience.'

Anna Russell says that founders must recognise when employees are wrong for the business. 'It's common for managers to um and ah even when they know in their heart there's a mismatch [but] the longer you leave it to get rid of them, the worse it is for everyone. Most employees will operate in a businesslike way and will have little time for those who don't perform or have wrong attitudes. Consequently, the respect they have for those who run the business will diminish if those people are left within the company.'

Simon Notley and **Robyn Jones** both stress the necessity for swift action. 'If you have an inkling that someone is not up to it, bite the bullet and get rid of them and don't mess around because you are so busy,' says Notley. 'You have got to get rid of them, you have got to make the time. It may inconvenience you to have nobody in the job, but it's short-sighted to keep someone on if they're not right.' Jones adds: 'As soon as you identify that someone is not right, get them out because the longer they're with you the more the problem will spread like a bad apple.'

What do you do if an employee is a friend? Be very cautious, says **Simon Needham**. 'When the markets collapsed in the late eighties, that had a big impact on our business via our clients. We had to get rid of five or six people. What we learned was that, if you don't do it properly, you get taken to court and you pay money. We didn't go through the right processes: we thought it was going to be fine and we were friends with people and they would accept the problems of the business, but you have to take it out of the realms of friendship. We definitely became more cautious because of that experience.'

> **20/20 . . .** 'Be nice and be tough. If an employee is not worth keeping, get them out – soon, because they bring the rest down.'
>
> – Jan Van den Berghe

Pick good people early on and they may become future leaders of the business. A number of **Jonathan Elvidge**'s employees joined him while his retail venture was small, and grew into bigger jobs. 'Most of the key people here have grown up in the business. The thing I have learned is to get the best people you can afford. If you imagine paying someone £20,000, what you effectively get is most of that person's life. It's hugely underestimated how much you can get from someone, yet they are probably the best asset you could have. Once you've identified the right person, you give them an opportunity. When you've shown that you have faith in people's ability, they return that investment significantly.'

> **20/20 . . .** 'The thing we've learned from all our ventures is to pick the best employees we could afford.'
>
> – Anne Notley

Motivating and delegating

Clearly, entrepreneurs need to motivate and develop the people they employ, and that often includes creating a place for them to move on to – which in turn creates impetus to grow the company. **Robin Hutson** says, 'We have always tried to spot talent and move it up, and one of the benefits of us opening more hotels is that there've been opportunities to move people on. 'Your staff can be motivated when you stop and spend five minutes showing interest in what they're doing. There was an event at the Savoy for the head waiter of the year, and our guy was third. The fact that he knew how busy I am, and yet would take a couple of hours out to support him, was all he needed for motivation for a couple of weeks.'

20/20 . . . 'Training our staff is vitally important. Even if we couldn't afford it in the early days, we did it.'

– Andrew Hobbs

Many people say motivating and developing staff is one of the most satisfying elements of running their own business. 'I absolutely love that buzz of trying to motivate and encourage people to reach their targets,' says one entrepreneur, 'making them feel good about what they are doing.' **Tim Connolly** believes good leadership is also about being able 'to anticipate issues before they are issues' – and **Aziz Cami** admits he frequently underestimated 'people issues' in the early days. 'I believed that staff were like me and would do whatever was needed, regardless of whether they liked it or had ability.'

James Sommerville says one secret of good management is to know when and how to show appreciation. 'Obviously in any organisation there are tiers and levels but just because someone is nearer to the bottom doesn't mean to say that they're not putting in as much effort. For two or three days, I did a stint as receptionist and it's a difficult job. Job swapping can be great: people can really appreciate how difficult that person's job is.'

And **David Landau** advises, 'Never stop questioning the people below you about what their life is like within the company. Never stop asking people who do theoretically menial jobs whether they are happy and treated well and paid well, and whether the job they're doing is a job they're proud of, or whether they wish they could find something else. It's absolutely crucial to keep asking those questions.'

20/20 . . . 'I come in most mornings to the factory just to check out things. I go down and say to people, "How's it going?" and that's also the bit I enjoy doing.'

– Simon Notley

As employees are motivated and developed within a business, they obviously need new challenges. Letting go of responsibility can be the difficult part for an entrepreneur, although some, like **James Sommerville**, say they enjoy it. 'We've always liked putting young people into positions of responsibility because that's exactly the position we were in when we were nineteen. We were doing grown-up men's jobs and were still only kids. We need to keep people who want to jump higher, so we have to make sure we put down higher hurdles, otherwise they will leave.'

Barry Bester observes, 'If you keep people down, they'll either leave because they want to progress, or you'll stifle them. You don't want your business to suffer when you go on holiday for three weeks, so you have to let go of these things. Not all at once – you don't give away the keys to the company overnight – but sometimes you have to let people get it wrong.' If you don't give your employees adequate freedom and opportunity, you may have to let go of them. Brett Gosper says, 'The mistakes we've made have been about letting good people leave or allowing a situation where a good person believes it's better to go to another agency. We've let four people go who are now running other agencies. You take it quite personally when someone leaves and when they are brilliant. In a sense, you think, "We really did miss out on keeping this person."'

However, sitting back and watching other people fumble their way through what appear to be simple jobs can be frustrating. **Robin Hutson** describes it as being 'like giving our baby away to the babysitter. It takes a bit of discipline to be able to stand back and let someone else get involved.'

> **20/20** . . . 'Business is very, very simple. It's people that complicate it.'
>
> – Neil Franklin

Jonathan Elvidge explains, 'When you're working in the first shop, you don't want to let anyone do the banking because you think it's only you that can do it. It's a skill that has to be learned. You let someone do the banking and they're quicker at it than you; they can add up better. You apply that principle to every single issue that affects the company, while at the same time trying to hang on to areas that are interesting.'

Shawn Taylor says that he is also training staff in how the business operates financially. 'In our game we're getting paid per hour, and you have to quote customers a time so if it takes longer, the job is costing you money. While another person roughly knows what they're looking at, I've done the job before and I've been there and I'm thinking, "Come on, let's get going." You're always tempted to jump in and push them out of the way and get the job done yourself. I've had to hold myself back hundreds of times.'

> **20/20** . . . 'I like to be busy but I don't like being a busy fool. I tend to delegate as much as I possibly can so I'm able to always take on more work.'
>
> – Julian Richer

To delegate is to relinquish an element of control, but, as **Ben Finn** points out, 'You can't do everything yourself.' Moreover, says, **James Keay**, 'You've got to see that things are not always going to be quite as you want.' After five years in business, he believes he is still too hands-on. 'I'm very intensive and thorough and the fact that I'm in the office most of the time makes it harder to let go – though it's also important to be close to what's going on. There are customers that I still personally deal with because . . . they have trust in me.'

One of the keys to delegation is to establish a firm chain of command. 'There are things that I just have to let go of,' explains **Robyn Jones**. 'I can't oversee everything. As long as I'm fed the information, it's OK. I just have to make sure my staff tell me the important stuff. It's wonderful when clients ask me, "What are you doing here?" That proves the rep is fulfilling their needs, and that to me is great.' As with many areas, the key is to combine autonomy with accountability as **Brett Gosper** describes. 'We don't mollycoddle people. We tend to hire very good people and let them get on with it . . . At the same time, there's the danger that they can feel a bit neglected. Some people want to be stroked and told what their career is. We're just not like that – but you've got to do a bit of that. At least, you've got to provide the belief that anyone can move up from where they are, that there are no glass ceilings and that young people won't get stifled.'

> **20/20** . . . 'People are what makes business fun. I mean, can you imagine playing a rugby match on your own?'
> – Colin Halpern

Some areas of responsibility are less easy to delegate than others. **James Millar** says that producing The Food Ferry catalogue, with more than three thousand lines and eighty suppliers, is a key area. 'Devolving the responsibility just doesn't work because the information gets out of kilter and we're producing something that we know is wrong. We could employ somebody to do it for us, but we feel we're blazing a trail here and we can't really rely on other people to do that in the same way.'

Millar has chosen to delegate in other ways. After several years based at headquarters in central London, he decided to work from home in Gloucestershire for two days a week. 'I don't like sitting in a room full of other people. I would far rather sit on my own and work things out,' he explains. 'I used to be stuck in the office and was always being asked, "Why isn't the water working?" and so on. I took the decision that these matters could be dealt with by people I was employing. If not, I'd employed the wrong people. Working from home, I can analyse the information that we generate from reports and statistics, and get a wider view of the market and start trying to apply this to our business ... Me scooting off down the M4 on Thursday evening and not being seen again till Tuesday afternoon did conjure deckchair images, but I hope I have now persuaded people that I still prop the place up from afar.'

> **20/20** . . . 'It's important that you involve people, not just boss them about, and never make people feel they are just doing the job.'
> – David Landau

Creating a company that works

Broadly speaking, culture is a word used to describe the way that people behave and interact. 'Companies are basically mini-societies and the values and the way people behave tend to cascade from the top,' says **Mark Jackson**, citing as an example 'the fact that I am sitting here in the office with my door wide open and that anybody in the building, any one of some hundred and fifty people, can and regularly do just wander in and ask me or tell me something'. In any company of more than two people, a culture will develop. One of the tricks to creating a successful business, says **Colin Halpern**, is to create an environment 'where people feel they are in it together'. To do this, 'you need to understand that the fact that you've been given an opportunity doesn't mean that the next person doesn't have the same dreams and desires and needs – even though they may not have the same abilities as you'.

Many entrepreneurs aim to create transparency in their office culture, a situation in which employees can make mistakes and own up without fear. But **David Landau** points out that he has known a number of companies whose manuals describe 'a kind of Utopia. You go into the company and you can perceive right away that the reality is far from that.' One way to increase candour, says Landau, is to use upward appraisals – asking staff to assess their managers. 'Listening to people and involving them outside of their own responsibilities is a very good way to make them feel valued. People who don't feel valued will never have any reason to do well in your company. My own appraisal was a very good lesson. Although I got a high approval rating, there were two or three things that people didn't like at all, and I changed my approach then and there. These appraisals make managers very careful to do what they say.'

> **20/20** . . . 'In order to be successful, you have to get the best out of other people. You have to have a formula where their interests run in common with your interests.'
>
> – Stuart Williams

Many entrepreneurs say endless meetings and tiers of bureaucracy left them frustrated with the corporate way of life, so it's not surprising that a start-up is often a fast-moving and exciting working environment. **Alex van Someren**, was 'quite determined to build a place that's fun to work in' and says he has no time for hierarchy. 'I try to make my secretary a cup of tea as often as she makes me one.'

> **20/20** . . . 'There's a myth about start-ups: that you have to kill yourself working twenty-five hours a day. I don't believe that's productive. We try to hire people smart enough to get their work done in fewer hours.'
>
> – Alex van Someren

Often small in numbers, start-ups can be uniquely flexible and informal. ATTIK has come a long way since its start-up days but **James Sommerville** says it has kept that 'can-do' environment and describes 'a fairly loose operation in terms of the way that we handle and manage our employees. If you've got to go somewhere at three o'clock, you don't have to go through layers of permission. You just go and come back and make sure your job's done. In a much more mobile world, people like to have freedom to make their own decisions and manage their own time. We don't have clocking on but we are small enough to be able to spot if the job's not being done.'

Many of **Arthur** and **Irene Allen**'s staff were married women coming back into the job market as children were growing up. 'Our approach was to be flexible and that's been rewarded with enormous loyalty, enthusiasm and great commitment,' says Arthur Allen. 'We built up the company with this group, mostly of women, often working part-time, all with great ability – one of those little undiscovered secrets.'

Sue Welland talks about creating 'a very different kind of culture' that values employees for their contributions outside the workplace as well as inside it. 'We have very carefully selected the staff, or they have selected us. One started up a hotel in Africa and found us on the Internet; another came to us from Australia; another was in advertising but doing an environmental project in their spare time. All of our people are entrepreneurs to a smaller or greater extent. They all have things they do outside the business, and that's great.'

> **20/20** . . . 'If staff aren't excited about what they're doing, they won't be able to convince anyone else.'
>
> – Richard Thwaite

Heather Rabbatts observes that employees can also enjoy a unique sense of ownership within the start-up situation. 'People can have a tangible connection to the product, which is rewarding – the sense of "I've built that". Everyone can share in the sense of achievement, whereas in large organisations you can feel a long way away from it.' And she reflects, 'I used to manage ten thousand people. Managing fifteen people is liberating.'

> **20/20** . . . 'A lot of people look at their success as being material success. But you only have to look at the finest chefs, the finest sportsmen, to see that success is never material – rather, it's the measure of their own ability.'
>
> – Neil Franklin

Nigel Legge and **William Carey** asked employees to choose between a pay cut and cutting staff in the early days because funds under management had been unexpectedly withdrawn. 'I think we learned from that difficult time the importance of involving all of those that were key in the decision making,' says Legge. 'Everyone who was a part of those early days found it stressful. We had expected to build on expectations and our principal desire was to build business, not to have to deal with a lot of complicated corporate problems. It rather buffeted us, but communication was key. We simply talked and talked and talked with all those among us that could contribute. I think that, now, everyone genuinely feels that they own a little bit of this, that our success belongs in part to them. Lots of people feel they genuinely have contributed to what is Liontrust.' He adds, 'If you get a reasonably able bunch of people working together, they make a big difference. If they don't work together, you may be facing disaster.'

Mark Smith and **Tim Connolly** knew they needed to engender more loyalty in workers as the company grew. 'Quite early, we took the decision to have a high proportion of employee ownership,' explains Smith. 'We were ready to dilute our stock in spite of the fact that many external advisers told us not to do it. Our view is that this is a people business and if people don't feel committed they will go. Do we want a small portion of a huge pie or do we want the biggest share of a small pie? Once you've got emotional issues out of the way, you can give bits away in order to make the business grow.'

David Abraham and **Andy Law** established a different model of ownership when they set up St Luke's but Abraham reflects that the theory of collective ownership did not always reflect the practice. 'Responsibilities were shared out but, as leaders, we were expected to take decisions. We were giving as much freedom as possible, but at the end of the day we had to worry about the big things.'

20/20 . . . 'People like the benefits of ownership but don't like the pressure that goes with the responsibility.'
– John Mortimer

James Sommerville says that his company's core is made up of several people who have been with ATTIK since its earliest days. 'Many of them joined us in Huddersfield in their early twenties when we were still a small blip on the map. There's definitely a sense of ownership in that respect, but obviously there's a need to bring in people that are new to the business too, people who are not part of the family. You can't have it all one way – you need that balance.'

QUESTIONS FROM THE EDGE

What kind of person enjoys working in a start-up?

Heather Rabbatts: 'On the whole, people who are interested in coming to work in a start-up environment are more open to the idea of taking a risk personally and professionally. They're also often in the early parts of their careers. Openness to learning is quite crucial: people have to be flexible, and prepared to see that something might have worked two weeks ago but now it's moved on. You can learn to cope, at one level, but some people prefer to seek regime and certainty while others thrive on ambiguity.'

At what point did you look for senior managers?

James Sommerville: 'We held off hiring senior people for a long time because we thought it might adversely impact the culture. We thought that, to everyone that joined, we were a cool design company and they would think, "Oh, no, they're getting all these serious suits in." But the shock never came. When we hired a chief executive, a financial director and a human-resources director, our people went, "Yippee! About time. Now I can knock on someone's door." '

How and when should I look for a nonexecutive director?

Anna Russell: 'In choosing a chairman, it's really important you find someone you can work with, someone who's not interested in being a mini-chief executive and will complement what you are trying to achieve.'

Simon Needham: 'Consider taking on an adviser on a temporary basis, for a day a month, somebody that's been not necessarily in your own business sector but in business generally, and is much more senior. An agency can find the right person for you. That's probably the best bit of advice I could give, because it will change your business for the better. We did it when we were five or six years into the business.'

What are the best ways to motivate and retain staff?

Nick Austin: 'The key to retaining people is to give them plenty of freedom in their job to contribute and feel their contribution is valued, even outside their regular area of work. The second thing is to offer big performance incentives so that people understand that they share in the upside of the company's performance and therefore they're not just a wage slave but effectively a shareholder. We very much involve people in the performance of the business – we sit them down every three months and tell them about what's been happening in the business, both the good stuff and the bad.'

What advice would you give on delegating?

Anna Russell: 'When you're in a start-up phase, everyone tends to get involved in everything but, as you grow, you need to have people at a senior level in place whom you trust to get on and make decisions. People with specialisms are there for a reason. Your business will suffer in the long term if you don't empower them. You just have to give jobs to a manager bit by bit, and eventually it becomes easier to delegate. Don't view delegation as dumping a lot of rubbish on someone else. You've hired that person because you respect their capabilities, so talk through things with them and get them to make decisions rather than assuming you have to carry everything on your own shoulders.'

ASSESS EIGHT

- The company may grow faster with more people on board, but may be slower to break even
- Before hiring at any level, write a job description
- Employ people who share your values and like getting things done – skills may matter less than attitude
- Hire people whom you get on with, not necessarily friends
- A nonexecutive director can help shape your growth
- Make sure a candidate will take your job if offered; if you make a mistake in hiring, put it right as soon as possible
- Employees are motivated by more than just cash
- Cultural values cascade from the company founders
- Recognise that employees have a life outside of work
- Give employees the right information to make decisions and if possible allow them to learn from mistakes
- Don't neglect to celebrate small successes

Quick list: In fewer than ten words outline

- The different stages at which you will need to recruit people
- How you will recruit
- Why people will join you
- Specialist or executive expertise you plan to hire in
- Qualities you will look for in managers
- How you will motivate and develop employees
- The areas you find hard to delegate
- Features of the culture you want to create
- How you can create a sense of ownership for employees

PART FOUR

WHAT'S NEXT?

Chapter Nine

How does a start-up get *grown* up? When is the right time to grow, and why? Is there an optimum size of business? What challenges does growth bring? Why and how should a business stay focused?

Why grow?

For many small businesses, the first years may be principally about survival rather than growth. Is there a right time to start pursuing growth? According to **Andrew Pollock**, 'the first year is relatively easy because you're full of adrenaline, you're new and people will always give you a chance. Year two is tough because you haven't got the resources and there's a temptation to expand because you thought everybody liked you – then you find they have gone back to their previous supplier. Year three is a struggle to make success certain. If you haven't got it right after three years, you're probably never going to. After that, unless you cock it up, you're away'.

Shawn Taylor also believes it takes three years to become established. 'People will try you out . . . By the third year, you get a reputation and things should start lifting off. The hardest thing is waiting for it, but that's also good: it keeps you pushing, keeps you on your toes.'

Growth can happen for a number of reasons, both reactive and proactive. For instance, a market grows rapidly and an ambitious company hires staff to keep up with the work, delaying break-even in favour of growing its market share. Another business has a successful product line and decides to capitalise on that by expanding the range. However, growth in staff numbers can give misleading signals if not matched by the bottom line.

Simon Needham remembers how 'to some degree, we over-employed in the early days. I remember thinking it was really impressive to see how many people we could employ. If we had thought, "Can we get two people to do an extra job between them?" the answer would have been "Yes", but instead we went out and got someone else. Doing business well is not about the amount of people you employ but about how much profit you're making.'

On the other hand, many companies are propelled into growth as a direct consequence of recruitment. **Colin Halpern** observes, 'The moment you stop growing is the moment you start shrinking because you cannot stay still – you need to retain people and give opportunities.' **Mark Smith** says that employing very good people means 'that the only alternative we have is to grow, otherwise they would get up and leave'; and **Aziz Cami** also makes a link: 'The only real reason you need to grow is to keep people, because, if you don't grow, there's nowhere to go and they will go somewhere else. Growth is all about people development.'

Why *not* grow?

What stops businesses from going for growth? One entrepreneur describes how 'for ten years we were desperate to keep the company small – we felt we were only as good as our weakest link'. **Jonathan Elvidge** also says that caution held him back. 'Growth was very slow at first: we were opening about four shops a year. Our slowness was based on the fact that we were a bit nervous about borrowing money from the bank. Perhaps if we had borrowed more and established a foothold in the market earlier, we would have less competition now.'

> **20/20** . . . 'A lot of people are unbelievably risk-averse and against change. All they really want is to be left alone to get on with what they were doing before. Unfortunately, that's a recipe for business failure. If you do nothing, your competitors will eat you for lunch.'
>
> – Roger Parry

Simon Notley and Mark Constantine both attribute early business failures to poor financial management and failure to understand the market. Before going into iron beds, Notley manufactured futons, but says that, at the time, people had started to buy furniture from out-of-town retailers. He had little capital and lacked faith in the product. 'It was all I could do because it was cheap to set up, but I didn't believe in it.' Constantine says he overpaid to get sales for Cosmetics to Go. 'We were getting customers but the catalogue [and] freephone were expensive and we weren't making a profit, even though we were doing an unbelievable amount of business. The strategy I had was exactly the same as for many Internet companies: "If we can grow this enough, we will move to profit." It was phenomenally successful but cost a lot to get sales.'

When liabilities become bigger than assets, a company is trading insolvently. While it's important to face realities, one entrepreneur who wound down his business says it's possible to create last chances. 'If you get into difficulties and are fairly honest, the bank will ask an insolvency practitioner to come in and do a study on the business. Your eventual success in turning it round may come down to whether the bank stays with you, so you must influence the report to be positive. An insolvency practitioner can pick up a contract by saying, "I think you will go under" – so insist that the report is done by someone else.'

Sometimes growth is slow because entrepreneurs are so focused on details that they miss opportunities. Sonita Alleyne remembers how 'long-term contracts gave us time to be heads-up directors instead of being heads-down and thinking about week-on-week and month-to-month progression. We had the ability to look over the parapet and say, "Where are we going?" ' Liz Meston reflects, 'It took too long for us to come off the shop floor and get our act together. But it was the problem of finding the right person to leave the job to. We've now got a full-time secretary but before that we were doing everything ourselves. As we were getting more franchises, we had to be more efficient because we realised we were being held back.'

How many people?

For some firms, keeping the head count small can be an effective way to maximise profits and maintain speed and efficiency. Andrew Pollock's vision is 'to stay focused and small. My view is that it's difficult to be a medium-sized business – the most successful businesses are the large and the small. The medium are just that: medium and mediocre.'

Jonathan Kennedy and **Andrew Macpherson** grew their business to more than fifty people but eventually sold their management arm and cut numbers back. 'We're determined to stay small,' says Kennedy. 'I would rather meet clients than be attending pointless meetings. I don't think either of us wants the crowding of space which comes with running a big empire.'

> **20/20** . . . 'With the right tools and ammunition, you can beat someone even if you're half their size.'
>
> – James Sommerville

Liontrust outsources as many functions as possible. 'Our view is that fund managers can run an awful lot of money without too many other heads,' says **Nigel Legge**. 'We outsource all the things that are head-count intensive, and don't involve direct contact with our clients. This allows us to concentrate on what makes the company successful. For instance, we pay a certain amount per meeting for a company secretary, whereas, if you hire a company secretary full-time, it could cost you £70,000 a year.'

Moya and Alec Crawford also choose to outsource to keep costs low. 'Our salvage experience has taught us to be lean and mean. We're not a big team and it works very efficiently,' they say.

Nick Austin says that experiences of turning around Matchbox, his former company, shaped his attitude to hiring people at Vivid. 'Both Alan [Bennie] and I are haunted by memories of termination interviews . . . We've always been cautious about hiring people. Our business is volatile, so we've always felt that, unless we could offer employment in the long term, it was better to outsource projects. We use a lot of specialist people, who are quasi-employees. The great thing is that we get some incredibly talented people – free spirits that don't want to be part of a big organisation. If we did have a bad year we could pull in our horns without making anyone redundant from our own team. Because our company is just over fifty people it's small enough to have that family feel. I'm highly reluctant to grow it. I feel that if we grow much more we will lose that feel – people say it becomes a bit more impersonal and cliques start to spring up. I think we will use the existing business model and keep outsourcing as much as possible.'

Entrepreneurs who have grown their businesses to more than a hundred people say success and speed can be maintained in a company that is well-led and well-managed. **David Abraham** remembers how 'we got to the stage where we created two groups of fifty people and there were debates about whether that would split the company, but it proved successful. At a hundred people we split into three or four groups and it became difficult to move across to another group, so latterly we refragmented the groups, mainly in order to create further growth, because we wanted to ensure that those smaller groups had more room to grow.' The way to cope with growth effectively, says **Irene Allen**, is to build teams and keep internal structures small. 'If you make people feel valued on a small scale and give them control . . . you can keep that impetus.'

Becoming focused

Strangely, a crisis often precipitates true growth in a business. **Tim Gilbert** and **Martin Rutty** built their courier company to have a turnover of more than £2 million in the eighties but, when hit by economic downturn, realised they had over expanded. 'We'd bought eleven or twelve Volvo cars to start up a chauffeur service, something we couldn't afford when things slumped,' says Rutty. 'We had just moved to big new premises when our accountant said to us, "According to my figures, you're going to go bust in three months." He was nearly right – we lost twenty-five per cent of our turnover in a few months.'

The pair decided to make some big changes. 'Once we had made the decision to stay with the business, we cracked on and worked like crazy,' says Rutty. 'It was the hardest time of my life . . . for four nights a week I stayed in a camper van at the office. I ran operations and Tim was trying to get the finance turned around. We had to stop serving customers who hadn't paid us; we slashed overheads and increased prices. Some business dropped away and work became more profitable. That meant we already had our hatches battened before the worst of the recession happened: we could expand without eating into our reserves, and our acquisitions in the early nineties gave us the confidence and the vision to grow.'

Speed began to build market share nationally, asking other struggling courier companies to sell their businesses into the network. Rutty and Gilbert also developed new computer software to track deliveries. 'We realised we were too dependent on one location – we needed a network. Big corporations wanted a single point of contact,' says Gilbert. 'We set about knitting together the businesses Martin was buying and moved from a ragtag-and-bobtail business to developing measurable information which corporations could manage.'

> **20/20** . . . '[As directors] we used to go off on tangents because we would each have enough authority to do so. That was dangerous. We still have this entrepreneurial spirit but we now always sit down and go through business ideas very carefully. Four of us on the board will pull an idea to pieces, and it's much more democratic than before. If we don't agree on something, we don't go there now.'
>
> – Karen Haddon

Many companies expand as a defensive move. **Liz Meston** and **Juliana Galvin** wanted to create a chain to get ahead of potential competition. 'We were scared that someone else would take our idea because we knew it was a great one, so that was why we felt we had to get into London, and then into franchising,' explains Meston.

During the recession of the early nineties, **William Sargent** and **Sharon Reed** borrowed £1.6 million to expand their business, even though work had begun to dry up. 'We were a niche boutique, providing customers with only a small proportion of their material, and our competitors started to package our bit more cheaply,' explains Sargent. 'We felt we would come a cropper if we didn't invest in editing equipment, so we became a full-service operation.'

David Landau also chose to grow *Loot* during a time of struggle. 'It was not a deliberate move to go global: it was defensive rather than offensive. We had started to publish in England and were still struggling quite a lot – it was 1987. There were other papers around Europe doing very well and it was clear that they were looking at England as a good market to expand into. I felt threatened by that and wanted a show of strength, and to bluff my way to the top table.

'The way I thought of was to suggest that a consortium of larger publishers start a paper in Holland. The way I painted things was that we were doing so swimmingly that not only were we about to launch in other countries, but we would gladly take part in this venture. The reality was far from that and it took me a long time to convince my partners in *Loot* that this was a strategy worth the price.

'At that time, budgets were tiny compared to what they are now, so it was tens of thousands of pounds' worth of involvement for us. It was a huge amount of money, and meant delaying our break-even point by several months. But I felt very strongly that, if we didn't do it, these other publishers would come to England and rob us of a slice of the market. I don't know how true my fears were, but that was the starting point of my interest in other countries, and I realised fairly early, after having launched a paper in Manchester, that launching papers in other countries would be much cheaper.'

Zad Rogers and **Hamish Barbour** switched focus from programmes to profits, and began to develop a better understanding of their audience. 'We started to recognise that we had been committing huge amounts of energy and resources to editing our programmes, but were bad at making money because we would make the best programmes regardless of budget,' explains Rogers. 'We began to realise that television is a transient medium and that all we were doing was enhancing the value of the broadcaster.' The pair also felt they were putting too much pressure on employees. 'We felt we needed to be more responsible and saw the most creative thing we could do was create value in Ideal World. We began to set some parameters and develop an attitude of "if you want this, you pay for it".'

20/20 . . . 'One of the most difficult areas to manage is the desire to be deeply creative and knowing when to stop.'

– Hamish Barbour

Sonita Alleyne says that 'at one time our business was about making things for other people. We began to ask, "Where's the value in that? What's the value proposition?" We realised the value lay in the ownership of channels, services, rights and so on – and we looked to concentrate our business in that direction.' Similarly, **Jonathan Kennedy** reflects on how his modus operandi has evolved from the start-up years when 'I would rush around doing things and not think about making money. It was about volume, rather than profitability.'

After five years running a chain of bars together, **Roy Ellis** and **Neil Macleod** noticed that profits were falling short of expectations. 'Some chains were beginning to attract high ratings, yet there we were with our hodgepodge of sites. We had everything from live-band venues to a disco bar with a seventies theme,' says Ellis. The pair had both hit the age of thirty, and spent two days walking in the countryside to figure out what to do next. On their return, they organised a staff retreat and asked each employee to appraise their colleagues.

'That consultancy exercise definitely raised the game of many of our staff,' says Ellis. 'From then on, we had to take seriously our own commitment to the company. That exercise was probably the biggest turning point in determining our roles. I became the managing director, and Neil began to look at developing the company.'

David Stuart and **Aziz Cami** decided in the mid-nineties that they would grow their business, which employed about 35 people. 'We'd got to a size and a level at which I sensed that we were in danger of stagnating,' remembers Cami. 'We needed to regain ambition and drive. Ostensibly, we had everything going for us, but I felt we were resting on our laurels. We got a consultant in, and the upshot was that I went into a more overt leadership role while David took a creative director's role. We either had to get smaller and become a specialist boutique, or bigger and more professional.'

'We decided to grow when everyone else was contracting,' Stuart recalls, 'which felt quite contrary. Our growth spurt coincided with work we did for the merger of Europe's largest law firm, Clifford Chance. It was a colossal piece of faith on their part to take on a small company, but we achieved the goals and started to appreciate that we had the skills. It's like an Olympic diving competition: if you do a complex dive you stand a chance of getting more points than if you just do a flic-flac off the springboard. The next step was to convince our designers, who enjoyed a flic-flac of a morning, to work on something more demanding . . . We woke up one day and realised this was something we could carry on doing.'

> **20/20** . . . 'You have to recognise an opportunity and strike while the iron's hot to capitalise on what you've already achieved. If you don't, you'll always remain a small company and someone else will steal your thunder.'
> – Richard Allen-Turner

Arthur and **Irene Allen** grew Listawood by spotting potential for products and innovating in related markets. 'When we started making promotional magnets, our competitors would take two or three days to provide a quote for their customers. We developed programs that allowed us to quote for any size, shape and quantity while the customer was waiting. That transformed the business, because, once a customer had got a price, they could buy. They didn't want to shop around,' says Arthur. In 1994, the company seized another opportunity when a smaller company asked for help in getting rid of bubbles from laminated materials. Staff at Listawood used foam pieces stuffed with dressmakers' pins, plus an old-fashioned mangle, to produce bubble-free computer mouse mats. 'We cleared the village store out of pins and rescued sixteen thousand mats, and that's how we got into manufacturing mouse mats.'

Challenges of growth

Getting growth right means hiring the right people to grow the business – but it's not always so easy or obvious. **Karen Haddon** says six years of financial struggle made Le Maitre reluctant to take on more staff. 'For years after our problems in the early nineties, we were very risk-averse. We had people doing three or four jobs until recently, when we realised that people should have one job and focus on doing it well. What convinced us was that we weren't growing. The millennium year was massive for us and we decided that, if we wanted to keep that turnover, the only way was to invest in people being out in the field. It's a hard lesson to learn, but, unless you invest in order to expand, you're not going to move anywhere.'

Marshall King and **Jan Van den Berghe** grew their companies rapidly and both recommend hiring key people as early as possible. 'It typifies the first-time entrepreneur that you don't recognise the needs you're going to have, and try to get by without necessary resources – until you realise you needed them three months ago,' explains King. 'I put off the need to appoint a financial controller and a general manager because I wanted to be prudent – at that point, it seemed we didn't need those extra people. Suddenly, we did need them and it was several months before we could get them into position. If I had my time again in starting up a hyper-growth company, I would recruit a chief financial officer at the outset, plus a human-resources director, because these people really help to direct growth. Spending time to recruit people seems like time away from what you should be doing, but it's actually the most important thing you can do. Entrepreneurs have a tendency to do everything themselves, but finding right people will take you from A to B more quickly.'

Van den Berghe recalls, 'We neglected the human-resources function and allowed miscommunication to creep in as we grew from eight to twenty-five. During our refinancing we were not in the office much and the soul of the company was gone. When we came back, things were different – small things, people not feeling happy, touchy-feely stuff. When we appointed someone as human-resources director, she got feedback straightaway. There is often a lot of stuff that people don't want to tell the founders of a company, but they still want it fed back anonymously. We never realised, for instance, that people might want loans for train tickets.'

> **20/20** . . . 'When you're planning to expand, get your people in before you start your expansion programme.'
>
> – Barry Bester

As a company grows, employees may begin to resist the changes in structure. **Mark Smith** observes, 'The paradox is that everyone believes that to grow you have to sacrifice your culture and values. A lot of problems centre on what people think it means to be big or bigger. They assume that, as you grow, you automatically create bureaucracy and no longer think important the things you once thought important.'

Good communication processes are vital for healthy growth, but how are they built? **David Landau** explains, 'You have to treat people as if you are still in a company of three, even if there are three thousand of you. The only companies that really work are those in which there's constant dialogue between management and the rest of the staff, and in which people feel they are . . . really part of the decision-making process. When you implement principles using other people as managers, make sure that those people are not only paying lip service but also believe the principles – to the extent that they spend time checking whether they're being followed, or whether they're just something on a piece of paper. Make sure they believe . . .

as passionately as you do, and are convinced that the best way of making the company work is by passing on those beliefs.'

Growth may be the goal, but its results can be difficult to adjust to: suddenly unfamiliar people are doing unfamiliar projects, and new layers of decisions need making. **Alex van Someren** comments that you need to 'do stuff to keep people together', and he adds, 'We do have a highly inclusive management style and encourage the idea that everyone should join in. Everyone has an opinion, which makes my job harder, but it does mean that the likelihood of my making a bad decision is unlikely to get through.'

Adam Twiss says, 'We never meant to be more than eleven people – that was all we felt we needed.' But he adds that, when a small company wins new ground, it often needs more staff to defend it. 'When you are two or three people, you can take on the world. You might be small but you're highly efficient and motivated. As the company gets bigger it takes longer, if you make a mistake, to check decisions and change courses, so you need to be a bit more careful. The stakes are a bit higher compared to just two of you in a student bedroom.'

It's vital for company founders to stay in touch with operations, he says. 'I make a big effort to walk around to talk and listen to a lot of people so they feel their talents are making Zeus work. My passion is not to be a manager of managers – I am much more interested in trying to shape the direction of our business and to keep the culture and drive and motivate people within the company. I speak to our salespeople because they are the people who are speaking to our customers. You can get more from speaking to four or five people about their conversations than by having them yourself.'

James Sommerville at ATTIK speaks of improving horizontal communication. 'We have tried to cross-fertilise designers and these days we have people from up to ten different countries working in one office. Ultimately, what we would like to do is get every person together – we talk about meeting up in Mexico and getting people on the beach to brainstorm and hang out, so that they don't just become email addresses but are real people to each other. It might cost us £100,000 but would probably return us that in a couple of weeks with the energy it would create.'

> **20/20** . . . 'It's not necessarily easier to cope with the money side as you get bigger. You have a better standard of living and are more seriously regarded but you have to invest substantial amounts of money in the business.'
>
> – Will King

Financial controls must become more sophisticated, says **Simon Notley**. 'In our first five years with the Iron Bed Company, our financial controls were useless. I had great intentions and learned lessons from previous businesses, and we did our best, but we didn't have the right people managing the accounts. We were rapidly expanding, and because we had reasonably good margins it wasn't crucial to count every last penny. Having good margins was probably one of the reasons for the success of the business – they buffered us against inefficiencies in management. It's taken us a long time to get our controls and infrastructure in place.'

James Sommerville reflects on the growth period when ATTIK opened two or three new studios around the world. 'We were on a roll and the economy was virtually telling us to expand. But, at the end of that, I went round to all five studios and the fax header was different for each one because the designers thought they had the licence to do it. We hated the word "process" but it was the fundamentals we needed to bring into line.'

> **20/20** . . . 'Entrepreneurs often start things but don't see them through, and, while instinctive touch and feel have much to do with the business in its formative years, the further you go, the more you have to rely on procedure and discipline as the business grows.'
>
> – Philip Newton

Is it necessary to institute formal processes, or are there other ways to manage growth? **John Mortimer** believes in a nonintrusive management style. 'Newly recruited senior people come in and say to me, "John, you've got a lousy organisation" and I say, "Actually, you're wrong. We have no organisation at all. It's specifically designed that way." It's like a commonwealth of independent countries who decide to get together because it's in their interest.

There's a lot of independence and autonomy as well as a requirement for co-operation but the balance is a judgment call for each individual. If people start to try to become corporatist, we have to break it up. In a meeting someone might say, "This is a good idea, John. Why don't we make all the people in the company do this?" or "I think it's a good idea, but I'll only do it if everyone else does it." Clearly, we have to support new ideas but we cannot force them on autonomous people.'

In some situations growth means that an entrepreneur's passion becomes diluted, standards slip and innovation evaporates. The challenge lies in managing scale, says **Roger Myers**. 'It's not hard to sort out a pub – if it's got smelly toilets and dirty seats and an unfriendly barman, you don't have to be a rocket scientist to know what to do – but just doing up a bar is only twenty per cent of the work. The difficulty lies in co-ordinating it all. Getting the standards right, getting people who have done something one way for fifteen years to change – to just communicate with so many people about what you are trying to do is very difficult. I could easily say, "Let's have cold beers in tall glasses" and you would think that's relatively easy. In a large organisation, what you might actually get is warm beer in round glasses. By the time it gets to the bar, you will find somebody hasn't listened or doesn't agree with the idea.'

> **20/20** . . . 'I have this little mantra in my mind all the time: "faster, better, cheaper". It's borrowed from some American management guru, but it seems to work.'
> – Nick Austin

Brett Gosper warns against becoming too safe. 'To get really good work out of an agency you have to test a relationship with a client and stretch your credibility. It's easy to say, "You are right" or "I'll tone that down a bit", whereas, if you keep forcing edgy solutions, you put the relationship under strain that the client is not comfortable with. It's highly risky, and sometimes we have not been as difficult as we could have been. In the early days the slightest thing you do, people say, "It's different." As you reach several years in business, you get to a stage where you don't have to worry as much or put in the hours that you did at the beginning. It's more difficult to maintain momentum because you're less hungry and you don't have that novelty factor.'

20/20 . . . 'Do not assimilate into the mainstream of thought and behaviour of the industry you are trying to revolutionise. An outsider has a crucial clarity of thought that has served him well.'

– Jeremy Seigal

A growing business needs to find ways to stay speedy and responsive as structures change and begin to solidify. What's right for the business last year is not necessarily right for the business this year, says **William Sargent**. 'If you avoid the fact that some people don't have the right skills and people aren't being retrained, in the end you'll have to make them redundant.'

As **Adam Twiss** says, 'When you're just starting up, you do tend to think, "We can take on the marketplace." When there's a new market and you're doing everything, it's all relatively simple, but markets get more complicated and people require more in terms of functionality, and you end up having to trim the amount of messages in a product. As you get more customers, you get more involved in mission-critical situations and you can't keep changing your products quite as much as you want to. In the last year or two, there's been a big change in our business and in the way that we sell our offering. We started selling a technical product in a technical way to solve relatively complicated problems of early adopters, but the costs are now more driven by business than technology drivers, so we got to the position where we were selling complicated products and the buyers didn't understand the problems.

'The shift in focus has been towards a solutions sale – saying to the customer, "We understand your problems, here's our credibility, here's a solution." We started to get involved in larger-scale corporate deals and felt that going in and presenting our technology was simply not working. What the customer wanted to know about was our credibility, and where the cost savings could be had, and how we were going to solve their problems. We had to scale our sales force so that we could simplify the sales message but still provide answers to complicated questions. The key is to make sure that you're flexible.'

> **20/20** . . . 'If you say, "This is our strategy for the next three years" and then blinker your eyes and go for it, it's a dangerous way to run a business.'
>
> – Mark Jackson

Staying focused

One common temptation for people whose businesses are fast-growing is to expand into unrelated areas of business. However, experienced entrepreneurs such as **Julian Richer** and **Colin Halpern** say that to diversify is often not a wise move. 'I do believe one should stick to one's knitting and only change if one hits a brick wall,' says Richer. Halpern adds, 'To me, diversification is like saying that my core business is no longer one that's dynamic. It's the kiss of death.'

> **20/20** . . . 'Your horizons do expand as you grow, but at the same time they also contract in a strange way.'
>
> – Adam Twiss

Howard Leigh was offered the chance early on to swerve from his original vision of providing a service to vendors of businesses. 'Within a month of starting, a buyer offered us a retainer to find deals. It was £20,000, and we were very tempted, but we decided not to take it. We've thought about working for buyers but came back to the conclusion that it's not in our interests. We have kept our focus on being a vendor-only business. We are good at selling businesses and we have created a niche.'

Jack Morris tells of how, in the early eighties, the group run by his family decided to buy an electroplating company, thinking this would complement its shop-fitting business. 'Part of our business used chrome-plated fittings and we were using a supplier and thought this was an opportunity. We thought, "We're good at shop-fitting, we could be good at electroplating." But it was a disaster and after a couple of years we sold the business to the management. It was just not for us. We basically didn't understand the market dynamics of the sector as well as we did the dynamics of shop-fitting. The proportion that we accounted for as a customer was not as material a part of the business as we had envisaged . . . [and] we were chasing external turnover in a very competitive market.'

The group went on to buy the old Royal Agricultural Hall in Islington and transform it into the Business Design Centre, but Morris points out, 'If it had all gone wrong, it could have made a huge dent in our organisation and set us back years. We decided that this kind of diversification was not a model for growing our business and now when we look at a business opportunity it is ring-fenced to an acceptable level of risk.'

> **20/20** . . . 'The crunch issue is about monitoring where growth is coming from to make sure that we don't continue to invest in areas that aren't coming up with the goods.'
> – Karen Haddon

Entrepreneurs are opportunists and optimists: they must also learn to say no. **Julian Richer** says, 'I've backed many start-ups with a pretty dismal record of success, as I think is the norm. I'm now very wary of start-ups – you know, people starting from scratch with grandiose ideas and no money of their own.' **Alex van Someren** believes his father was less successful than he because 'he tended to move from one thing to the next without remaining focused. There are some upsides – when one thing looks less good, you can switch to another and get away with surviving through tough times – but it's a defocusing.

'We turn down a lot of people who say, "You must be interested in my new improved padlock or my anti-hacker device." No, we're not. It's not nearly interesting enough just because it has to do with security. There are lots of aspects of security: we are only in one of them, and we are staying in one of them. The area we work in is very tightly defined indeed and that surprises people but it also prevents us from dissipating our energies. I think focus is incredibly important.'

QUESTIONS FROM THE EDGE

What are the benefits of growth?

Colin Halpern: 'Growth is exciting: it's like being able to run faster and faster. It's what keeps people motivated. It stops people bickering because they are totally engaged in the process of how they can make the business grow. It's exciting stuff – you want to get up in the morning and go to your place of business, because, along with the usual challenges, there are other exciting and out-of-the-ordinary things to do.'

What have you learned about fast growth?

Andy Hobsbawm: 'It's so difficult to maintain quality when you are going for hyper-speed growth. Realise that at the start and promise less – temper the ideal about what you might do if you had the time, money and resources, and figure out what promises you really can deliver on.'

What are key advantages of being a small company?

David Abraham: 'If something needs to be done, you do it. You tend not to worry about implications as much. In a larger company, there are often a lot of issues around permission. People might have ideas but feel that they're not fully entitled to go with those.'

Robert Eitel: 'We can be responsive and change quickly if there's something wrong.'

As you grew, did you keep the 'start-up' mentality?

Anna Russell: 'We're no longer a start-up but we still nurture an element of that mentality. You do need to start putting in processes but it's also important to maintain a sense of nimbleness and can-do. Some companies do that by keeping small and not having more than a couple of hundred people in one place. It's mainly making sure you communicate well . . . and that people understand decisions. When you're a start-up, you have that energy of a shared goal, a shared vision, and it's important to sustain momentum and common purpose. We've introduced think-tank meetings throughout the business, where people from all departments talk about key areas, good ideas and feedback.'

Have you resisted taking opportunities in other sectors?

Simon Notley: 'At long last having found something successful that I enjoy doing, why go and dabble in other things that I don't really know about?'

Will King: 'Constantly, opportunities come along which divert your mind off the main goal. You entertain them; you think, "A few years ago, I would have done that." Even so, in a hundred ideas you get presented with, one will be really good, and I'm very loath to turn down an opportunity to take something that's going to be big.'

Mark Constantine: 'You are always going to get diverted. I would recommend being diverted. But I have never been very good at anything but cosmetics, and things allied to that.'

ASSESS: NINE

- Growth is necessary just to stay still
- Employees are often motivated by growth
- Keeping head count low can help maximise profits
- Lack of market intelligence, bigger-picture vision and focus can all hinder growth
- Financial controls must keep pace with head count
- Growth doesn't have to entail bureaucracy
- When looking to diversify, don't think you can succeed in any market. Stick to your knitting if possible

Quick list: In fewer than ten words, describe

- What holds back growth in your company
- What would spur growth in your company
- Your desired rate of growth
- Your goals for growth
- Your recruitment strategy for growth
- How you will maintain standards
- Potential pitfalls as your business grows

Chapter Ten |

How do small businesses move into a bigger league and how do entrepreneurs adjust to the change? What are the challenges of raising new funds and entering new markets? What is it like to sell a business and say goodbye, or stay involved under new leadership? What causes people to start up from scratch again?

New funds

A thriving small business has several options for growth into a larger business. Some people choose to grow their businesses by reinvesting profits over the years, but many will look to raise more money, either through a longer-term loan or development capital from outside investors. Another option is to seek a listing on the Alternative Investment Market (AIM) or on OFEX, a privately owned trading facility for smaller companies not listed on the main exchange.

Mark Smith observes, 'There's no doubt that, if an organisation wants to grow reasonably fast, it has to raise money. Lots of people are willing to give you money and each comes with their own set of strings. If you are going a different route and floating, you need to be clear about the external disciplines . . . the expectations of the marketplace are such that you are not always allowed to do the things for the business you really want to do.'

After several years in business, **Simon** and **Anne Notley** began looking for an investor with the aim of raising money to open Iron Bed Company shops at a faster rate, and also to take their own money out of the business. 'Anne and I are not very patient people and we have a large mortgage, which it would be nice to pay off,' says Simon. After considering venture capital, the Notleys opted to take out a longer-term loan. 'Realistically we can raise a couple of million without giving anything away because we make reasonable profits. If we want to keep full control of the company, we've realised we can't get money out at the moment. We're not desperate; we have the luxury of time.'

Similarly, **Nick Austin** wanted to release some of the money he and colleagues originally invested in Vivid. They chose to go with a venture capital firm based in New York. 'There's an adage that the Atlantic Ocean is a fine invention and for us that's proved to be the case – it means they can't micromanage us. We see them three times a year for board meetings and give them management accounts every month and that's about all the interest they show in us. We felt that the benefit with these guys was that they seemed very hands-off and they really believed in [the] management – in us and in our abilities.'

Sonita Alleyne and **Jez Nelson** sold a ten per cent stake in their company Somethin' Else in spring 2001 to raise money to finance expansion. 'About five years ago, someone tried to buy us but they put a cap on the value of the company, so we didn't go for it,' says Alleyne. 'We have had a few people over time wanting to buy us or get a stake in us, and we haven't liked the idea of it, because there's an emotional stake in running a business. Nor were we ever planning to sell the whole company, because there's so much opportunity. The first time you get an offer, you think about the future and "is it the right decision to sell?" It's not a question of "oh, it's my baby" but it's the fact that I am in control of my life and no one tells me what to do. The issue is "what control will someone have over me?" We have never had anyone telling us we can't do things.'

Kevin Bulmer decided to list his company, Synthetic Dimensions, on OFEX after considering investment from other sources. 'We went some way down the line with an offer which was very serious and fitted with our development ideas. We realised then that if we sold the company, we would lose control. In theory, you look at the company and say, "It's our baby." But it wasn't really so much that which stopped us: it was more that we felt the plans which the potential buyers had for the company weren't making the best use of the facilities that we have. The missed opportunities seemed ridiculous. We had the skills to do these things and, really, there was so much more that the company could be. We needed an opportunity to achieve the same level of funding but without losing control, and the only way to do that was through a flotation.'

Barry Bester and **Stuart Williams** floated Topps Tiles on London's main stock exchange. 'I would not have been happy with seeking venture capital,' explains Bester. 'Venture capital is great for management buy-ins and buy-outs because you're looking at people with no money of their own. But as an owner of a business you would find it galling to give away a very large percentage and would have to ask, "Are their aims the same as mine?" A venture capitalist would want a short- to medium-term exit.' Bester calls flotation 'the best thing we ever did' but adds, 'It will not suit every person. You have to remember you cannot do what you want: you have to be fair to your shareholders. I don't decide what I earn: a remuneration committee decides it for me. I can't just do exactly what I like.'

New markets

While there are pitfalls in diversifying too widely too quickly, most entrepreneurs are keen to capitalise on existing success. **Jonathan Elvidge** learned from watching Sophie Mirman's Sock Shop in the eighties that, once a company has created a niche for a particular kind of product, it's not long before other, larger companies jump on the bandwagon. 'We're in a similar situation but luckily we're strong because we've grown slowly, have good buying power and a very efficient team,' he says. 'When there's a bit of pressure on revenues and a drive to compete and the market is diluted, only the strong survive.'

Sue Welland and **Dan Morrell** also speak of branching into non-tree areas. 'We're evolving into the Future company, going into non-forestry offset and carbon credits,' says Welland. 'We have a skill in translating complex environmental problems into something which consumers can understand and companies can promote, and at the moment that's global warming, but, on a five-year-plus scale, I don't know what the next thing will be.'

Helphire established another division after seeing a niche for legal-expenses insurance, but **Mark Jackson** says, 'We don't see ourselves diversifying widely. We are constantly looking for new ways of doing business, but our core skills are call centres, service provision, replacement vehicles and legal services.' After more than ten years in business, Speed Couriers branched into selling mobile phones and contracts to its business users. 'It's something we have used our experience in the industry to sell,' explains **Martin Rutty**. Avalon added related divisions to its core business as it saw opportunities. **Jon Thoday** says, 'We branched into promotions because no one wanted to promote our acts, and into television to build a team around our artists; plus, we fired so many public relations companies that we thought we might as well start our own.'

> **20/20** . . . 'If you want to roll something out, the big trick is simplicity. If you're doing a lot of it, it has to be simple.'
> – Roger Myers

Entrepreneurs in the retail sector may decide to roll out their concept through creating a franchise package, but **Colin Halpern** warns that 'becoming a franchiser is to take on a tremendous responsibility – it's taking people's hard-earned or borrowed money and putting it into business, so I think you have to believe in your heart of hearts that you are doing the right thing. Franchising should not be a way of trying to pass off the risk on someone else.'

The founders of The Curtain Exchange opened a shop in London, and began getting several queries from people interested in running a franchise. One early experience, when a 'franchisee' decided to leave the alliance and set up on her own after three months, left them cautious. 'We weren't ready for it. We were naïve,' says **Juliana Galvin**. 'It was a real kick in the stomach and it made us ask, "If we're going to have other shops, what would be the best route?" ' Galvin and her partner, **Liz Meston**, went on to devise a package and to build a network of franchises in the UK. 'We would have needed a lot of money to open all our own stores,' explains Meston. She says relationships with franchisees can still be tricky. 'It's difficult to say to people, "You have to do this." We try to keep in contact but, once they get into the swing of things, we don't have that hold on them.'

> **20/20** . . . 'Opening offices is not that difficult; managing offices is where the skill lies.'
> – Simon Needham

Franchising may be a way into new markets abroad. The Lush retail concept was so successful that its founders began to be inundated with requests from people wanting to set up branches around the world. 'Some Canadians said, "We want to do this in Canada. We'll pay to do it and do the manufacturing as well." That was the deal we came up with, and we had some of their shares,' says **Mark Constantine**, who receives several hundred enquiries each year. 'If you can create enough excitement, people come to you and want to be involved and they're likely to want to pay for it. It's not high-risk for us, because we didn't put anything into it, other than our expertise. It's not difficult to get a roll-out right, it's just hard work.'

Foreign markets are generally tough to capture, and, as **Colin Halpern** says, 'If you are not a major player in your home market, why go somewhere else? Why don't you work hard to turn your five per cent market share into fifteen per cent?'

However, for **Jeremy Seigal**, rolling out The Perfume Shop into mainland Europe is a vital next step and a key plank in strategy. Having established a base of stores in the UK, he aims to double that number in the next five years and drive consolidation of the European fragrance retail market. 'Despite our growth to number-three retailer of fine fragrance in the UK, with a ten per cent market share, it's our position against other European retailers that will matter in the long run,' he says. 'Seeking to be a UK player alone is not sufficient.'

Silicon.com was circumspect about entering markets abroad, spending two years building operations in Britain before launching in Germany and France. 'Our aim has always been to get into the three biggest markets in Europe and to make sure that we build a business in those territories which is really solid before going wider,' says **Anna Russell**. 'Doing that always takes longer than you think.' Russell says businesses should concentrate on refining existing revenue streams, as well as developing new ones. 'We are broadening out our revenue streams, looking at where we derive revenue from and at how we can make that work better for us and our customers.'

Acquisitions

Some entrepreneurs grow their businesses by buying and integrating other companies. **Roger Parry** has bought many companies in the past decade and says acquisitions fall into two broad categories: strategic acquisitions, which take a business into a new geographical market or stream of business; and 'tuck-in' acquisitions, used to strengthen an existing position. Tuck-ins, or buying more of the same type of company, are relatively easy, says Parry. 'You can instantly look at a company and say, "The margins look very high." The risk of it going wrong becomes exponentially greater as you move outside your own industry.'

> **20/20** . . . 'Every acquisition has its price and sometimes the cost is too heavy in the business.'
>
> – Nick Austin

Small deals can be more trouble than big ones, he says. 'Frequently, with a small company, you are buying from an entrepreneur or a private vendor who may be better at concealing problems and extolling virtues, and may be a more emotional, difficult negotiator who will push to the last nickel.' Often, a public company is a safe bet. 'The discipline of being on the stock market usually makes it transparent. Those of us who make our living out of mergers and acquisitions will tell you that the best possible thing to buy is a neglected division of a large industrial corporation, where a lazy band of managers don't understand the business. Frequently, it's extraordinarily badly run: these are the places to get maximum value.'

The best deals are those where the management of the acquired entity are enthusiastic about their new parent. The worst type of deal, says Parry, is a small company bought from a venture capital firm. 'They will pump the thing to the absolute limit so there's nothing left for the purchaser. The only time when that doesn't happen is with tuck-in acquisitions, when something is worth more to me than it is to them.'

Parry also says that it's important to think about the psychology of the seller. 'With family firms, if you have a sensitive manner, you can sometimes do some spectacular deals. If you are a good deal maker you can do the same deal as your competitor on better terms because people trust you and like working with you. When people are selling to you directly, they won't always go for the deal that has the largest amount of cash on the table upfront. The trick of getting the deal done is to really understand what the other side is looking for. I have been asked, "Can I have a job for life?" or "Can I have a Mercedes?" or "Can I build a new office?" In some cases, the answer is yes.'

In deals done outside the UK, says Parry, make sure everyone is using the same currency, and take account of cultural differences. 'I've seen numerous acquisitions where people are poring over spreadsheets and they all have different numbers . . . When you're trying to do a deal in Spain, you have to live with the fact that everyone is going out for a meal at 11 p.m. and at 1 a.m. they want to discuss the finer points. If you're not prepared to do that, you won't get the deal done. If you're trying to do a deal in Germany, you have to accept the fact that you have to go to about five meetings before you can have a substantive discussion . . . Europe is not a homogeneous place when it comes to business.'

Selling up

David Landau sold *Loot* after he received an offer too good to miss in the autumn of 2000. 'I had been approached regularly and always put offers in a drawer and said, "The time will come when I will be ready to sell . . . I'm not ready yet." I probably would never have sold the company, but the Internet situation that arose was such that it was blindingly obvious to me and fellow shareholders that the bubble was going to burst. We were being offered so much for the company's potential that it was an opportunity that was not going to stay long or come back for some time. The price we were offered we felt was very high compared to what the company might have fetched earlier, so it was a question of opportunity to some degree, and also luck. We had many people saying, "You must be mad – selling it now", but obviously I came to the conclusion that the time was right.'

> **20/20** . . . 'I really believe in luck – it's part of the game and some people just don't have it. One knows if one is lucky; you know if your friends will get it right, or fall on their feet. With some people, it's just one bit of luck after another. But luck in itself is not enough. In reality, you have to work very hard for anything to work, but luck does help you to go one step further.'
> – David Landau

Daniel Gestetner sold a stake in his Internet company ShopSmart to AOL and Wal-Mart in the summer of 2000. When the market collapsed and chances of getting further investment became slim, he brought in Ernst & Young to manage the process of selling the business. Indigo Square, a joint venture between Barclaycard and Nomura, bought it in the spring of 2001. 'They saw it as an opportunity to gain twelve months on development by taking over a well-known brand,' explains Gestetner. 'It wasn't necessarily what I had planned, but the nine months leading up to the sale were a tough time and a lot of businesses were going bust. This sale meant the business could drive forward and most of the staff were retained.'

His motto is 'sell out, get out'. 'If you have sold a business which you were controlling, it's difficult to assume a role where you no longer have that element of control, to sit there and be part of a team. We were used to a fast-paced dynamic environment – we built a brand from nothing to the number-three dotcom brand in the UK and you can't do that with a bureaucratic structure around you. I didn't want to stay on full-time.'

> **20/20** . . . '[In selling] you need to be prepared for the consequences and the fact that you will lose control. You need to be ready for the business that you have built to be completely and utterly changed by the people who are buying. If you're not prepared, you will probably regret the decision to sell.'
>
> – Mark Smith

Selling up isn't simple, says **Nick Rose**. 'Deal-making is never done unless it's signed in blood. Handshakes aren't quite good enough. When we were looking to sell, one company offered a price that we were going to refuse, but even so we said, "We'll have that in writing, please." Next day, they responded with an email saying they didn't want to do the deal. The lesson we learned was to set up a strict timetable. We weren't confident enough to be firm with the people we were negotiating with. If we had said, "Let's exchange due diligence in three weeks' time and come to an agreement the following Friday, and have our solicitors draw up contracts a week thereafter" – yes, we may have been in danger of scaring that company off, but the probability was that they were not that interested anyway, so you can then move on to the next company. One of our board members always says, "If a deal can be done, it can be done quickly."'

> **20/20** . . . 'Everyone says they don't want to sell but everyone wants to sell at the right price.'
>
> – Liz Meston

James Millar spent several months talking with a potential buyer, but decided not to sell. 'It became clear that they were trying to install us as a new home-shopping department of their company. They portrayed that their understanding of e-commerce was greater than it really was and made out that we would be part of a team. It turned out there was no such team: we would become the team and would have to run the whole thing up and down the country, which was not what we wanted at all.'

He says that, in selling a company, 'you have to be deeply suspicious. If anyone approaches you, make absolutely sure that you understand what's happening from that person's point of view. Don't decide on something overnight; but, if you have to go through eight or ten months of talking, something is probably up.'

Staying involved

Andy Hobsbawm and **Eamonn Wilmott** merged their business Online Magic with Agency.com and stayed with the global group. 'When I started the New York office of Online Magic, hundreds of new media companies were shooting up all around us like skyscrapers,' recalls Hobsbawm. 'I felt we couldn't compete effectively, and this was part of the reason for doing the deal with [NY-based] Agency.com.' Wilmott became the head of Agency.com Europe and Hobsbawm its chief creative officer.

Far from stifling them, the move gave space to grow. 'Can you be entrepreneurial within a large structure?' asks Hobsbawm. 'Certainly. It's more a state of mind than anything else. It's about not settling for mediocrity, constantly kicking down the walls of bureaucracy and realising that the instincts which helped you survive in the first place are still worth following.'

Forward Publishing and FrameStore both brought in the Saatchi brothers as investors. **William Sieghart** and **Neil Mendoza** sold half of their business to release capital, but ended up buying it back. 'We wanted to take more control and we wanted to involve our management in ownership,' explains Mendoza. 'In an agency, that's vital these days, that people who do all the work need to own it.' In 2000, **William Sargent** and **Sharon Reed** also decided to buy back their business after several years as part of the group Megalomedia.

Not many businesses keep their founders for as long as Speed Couriers. **Martin Rutty** has been at the helm since he started the company at the age of nineteen. 'I think it's difficult to be entrepreneurial after twenty years in the same business,' he admits. 'In many ways, it's a bad thing to be entrepreneurial for that long. When you've got a stable and mature business what you need is a little bit of formula. As I've got older I've mellowed out, though that doesn't stop me from wanting to try things. Most entrepreneurs start with a pretty high energy level but as time goes on you do tend to become more philosophical.'

Stepping back

As a business grows, many entrepreneurs see that they need to step back from an operational management role. It's not easy to let go at first; one person describes it as being 'incredibly frustrating, like having your mouth Sellotaped'. **Charlie Muirhead** believes that positive personal chemistry between a founder and an incoming chief executive is crucial for such a transition to work. In early 1999 Ashley Ward was appointed as chief executive of Orchestream, after a period during which Ward was a consultant to the business.

'I used to have conversations with our chairman Alan Bates saying, "Alan, whenever you think you need to hire a chief executive, let me know,' says Muirhead. 'The reality is that spotting new ideas and being creative is something that you don't need a tremendous amount of experience to do, although I think experience helps. On the other hand, managing companies is something where experience is everything.

The challenge [of bringing in a new chief executive] is not insignificant because a company starts with a culture and usually the founder is passionate about making the company successful and understands how it came into being. The danger is if someone comes in with ideas, thinks they are right, and doesn't know some of the important issues. The number-one thing that's got to be right is the chemistry. You can't just find somebody with a great track record and expect it to work.'

> **20/20 . . .** 'It's clear that there are things we would do differently, but at the time all the decisions seemed right. They seemed musts.'
>
> – Nick Rose

Sue Welland and **Dan Morrell** spent five months looking for a new chief executive. 'We didn't want to run the business ourselves,' explains Welland. 'What we wanted was somebody who was a businessman working more generally in environmental consulting, someone that Dan and I could respect and work with and who could do the job more efficiently than us. I think that you can love the business so much that you forget how to run it and you lose your sense of objectivity. Someone who comes in from outside will be used to doing exactly that – being objective and running a business properly.'

James Sommerville and **Simon Needham** appointed a chief executive in 2000 with the aim of planning a new chapter in the life of ATTIK and opening more design studios around the world. 'We talk about pulling it together systematically,' says Sommerville. 'Before, we were like a teenager's bedroom and now we're like mum's front room. If we want to raise additional finance, any potential investor will come in and kick the tyres and if we're a mess they will get scared. We've put management teams and executives into each studio and we have stepped back – we don't want a dependency culture. We still do the same as we've ever done, but ten years ago we would have been picking up the phone and doing cold calls to companies in Leeds, whereas now there's an opportunity to network at a more senior level. You still have to make contact somewhere and it's important that we are seen out in the field of play, trying to lead by example.'

Neil Mendoza stepped back from Forward as he began to focus on other things. 'I don't really associate myself with this particular company any more. I've done my job here and it runs by itself. I think we want to leave it very fluid, very flexible. I've started a couple of things in other areas – for example, a business doing tax deals for films – and I don't want to set up another big business. I'm fed up with managing people. I'm a time freak and I don't want money. All I want is time and more of it, to be able to choose what to do with it. I am not the kind of entrepreneur that wants to build an empire. I get a kick out of starting companies and getting people to run them.'

In spring 2001 **David Abraham** left the agency he had co-founded to take a management position at the television group Discovery. He explains, 'I suppose there was a turning point in terms of my approaching my forties. St Luke's had kept me in the advertising business but, at the same time, I was beginning to explore ideas of what the company could be other than just an advertising agency. Andy [Law] and I could have spent every day talking about St Luke's as an idea but our income came from serving clients. It was not going to be practical or fair to try to reinvent the company around what I wanted to do, which was much more in the area of entertainment.'

Going back into a larger, more structured company offered him the chance to be more, not less, entrepreneurial, says Abraham. 'If anything, I've found the daily decision-making processes much more like those of an entrepreneur, whereas in an agency situation it's done on behalf of other people. [Here] it's more like piloting a plane and I actually feel more needed as a leader.'

> **20/20** . . . 'Some entrepreneurs do want to keep control and find it impossible to function in a corporate environment, but many entrepreneurs make the transition extraordinarily comfortably.'
>
> – Roger Parry

Starting again

It seems that people who start businesses fall into at least two camps: serial entrepreneurs who have several things on the go and are forever itching to put new plans into action; and those who say they would never want to endure the start-up period again. 'I think people who start another business must be mad,' says **Andrew Pollock**. 'Someone asked if I regretted leaving Ernst & Young and during years two, three and four, I would have replied, "Dear, dear, yes." From year five I couldn't imagine why I didn't do it earlier. I found partners looking at me and saying, "I wish I could do that." ' Pollock says his ultimate ambition is for the firm to outlive his own involvement. 'I would love in years to come for somebody to say 'We use Rees Pollock – they're very good. Are they any relation to you?" '

Speaking several months after leaving *Loot*, **David Landau** says that, at the time he sold, 'I didn't have my future all mapped out. I have already started to make plans ... but I know what a new business involves – I don't want to go back to working fourteen hours a day'.

Brian Clivaz says that he would start up another company tomorrow given the chance, 'because it's in my blood', but **Sue Welland** is conscious of the need to resist distractions. 'I definitely think that Dan [Morrell] and I would start another company together. I think there's too much here, though, and I'm not allowing myself to have another idea because it will distract me and I want to give this two hundred per cent.' **Nicola Murphy** talks about retiring as a millionaire at forty but admits: 'I don't know how we would give it up, really.'

Terry Pullen has started up several ventures over the years and describes how being entrepreneurial can become addictive. 'I adore the highs and lows that come with the job and I adore the fact that my destiny is down to me. Even though I've had to employ a lot of people, it's down to me which ones I employ and if they're good it's because I've recruited well. If you have made money or have made a successful business, then you will believe you can do it again. Therefore, why would you not do it again? If you've got through it once, you will do better the next time.'

QUESTIONS FROM THE EDGE

Is acquisition a good way to grow?

Jack Morris: 'Even if people stick to what they know, they get attracted to acquiring businesses that may have a synergy, thinking, "This could add value." Before you acquire something, you should think, "If I deploy the resources into my main business instead, could I get more profit out of my main business?" '

Nick Austin: 'We are developing so strongly organically that we look at something and say, "How much quicker can this take us up the curve?" Usually, companies are for sale because they're not working or because the founder or principal wants out. Chances are that you are going to dilute your own management forces. If we continue to grow organically in things that we

---

understand and things that we can make happen at our speed, maybe that's better than taking wild risks on a business we don't understand.'

What is it like to sell your business?

William Sargent: 'You can't overestimate how hard it is to go through an acquisition. It was painful selling our shareholding and completely messed up our life for the period. Don't imagine you're going to carry on running your business while someone is following you around doing due diligence.'

What was your experience of floating your business?

Alex van Someren: 'I found the initial public offering to be unlike what everyone was telling me, that it would be a big scary monster and leave me exhausted. I personally thrive on that sort of thing. It's busy and time-consuming but a lot of fun and we got a fantastic result.'

Barry Bester: 'The sad thing is that to get it right you need to do it more than once. You also need to do plenty of research. Don't go with the first set of advisers that you meet, and question why people are recommending them to you. Don't go to one of the really big advisers if you're a small company: go with someone that understands your market. Make sure you know your story, stick to it, and don't be frightened about being overenthusiastic. You have to convince these guys that you have got something that's really good and going to make lots of money. Don't have all your team going round doing the City bit because you will lose focus and, at the end of the day, the business is what's important.'

How can we prepare ourselves to sell our business?

David Landau: 'There are a lot of things in a company that, however well run it is, are not quite in the state that they should be. I'm talking about contracts, agreements and so on, implementations of things that you have signed the agreements for seven years ago and which don't actually happen. Everything has to be absolutely spick-and-span. You can't say, "That computer was never sent because Jack never got round to it" because that sends a lawyer freaking out.'

William Sargent: 'Get in extra help and take on extra people in your finance team. Try to spend the six months before the sale preparing due-diligence packs. You can anticipate that a buyer will say, "Give me your property details" and no one is going to buy your company till you get to that stage. At that point, it starts costing you money because the tab is running with the professionals who are involved in the sale. If you get all the work done at your leisure by getting in temps, when someone comes along, it's all in the cupboard and you can say, "There's twenty-five files, all photocopied, you're welcome to walk away with them." The buyer will be gobsmacked.'

Should I leave the sale of my company to the professionals?

William Sargent: 'The meter is running, so any delay upgrades the costs. If you have ten professionals in there at £200 an hour each, it's pricey. You do have to control people. Let accountants run with the ball but remember that, if you let them negotiate on your behalf, quite correctly they will try to win every point. The reality is that there are things that are important to you, and if you go away and leave the responsibility to your professionals, and don't make your decisions till the end of the process, it will take longer and be more expensive, whereas if you stay in the room with them it will cost you less. You don't need to go down the contract line by line or through all hundred clauses – but you can say, "These three points are important." '

ASSESS TEN

- All investors come with their own set of strings attached
- Flotation brings restrictions of its own

- Your horizons expand as your business grows, but also contract as you accumulate customers
- It can be a mistake to diversify if there is still a large amount of growth in your core business
- Look for related areas where there are synergies with your core business
- Refine existing revenue streams as well as developing new ones
- You may not be the right person to grow your business to the next level

Quick list: In fewer than ten words, outline

- Your options for funding growth
- Advantages and disadvantages of each route
- Potential areas or markets for expansion
- Experience or knowledge of those areas
- Your endgame for the business
- What your job will be in three years' time

Useful Addresses

www.britishchambers.org.uk general business news
www.businesspages.co.uk business search engine
www.cim.co.uk Chartered Institute of Marketing website
www.dti.gov.uk Department of Trade & Industry website
www.hmce.gov.uk Customs and Excise website
www.kompass.com business to business search engine
www.startups.co.uk gives case studies, guides etc.
www.taxguide.co.uk gives details of the Enterprise Investment Scheme
www.tec.co.uk Training and Enterprise Councils' website
www.thomweb.co.uk business search engine

Association of British Insurers (ABI), 51 Gresham Street, London EC2V 7HQ; Tel: 020 7600 3333 (www.abi.org.uk)

The Bankruptcy Association of Great Britain and Ireland (gives advice on bankruptcy, how to deal with it), 4 Johnson Close, Abraham Heights, Lancaster LA1 5EU; Tel: 01524 64305 (www.theba.org.uk)

British Venture Capital Association, Essex House, 12–13 Essex Street, London WC2R 3AA; Tel: 020 7240 3846 (www.bvca.co.uk)

Business Link. For local link, tel: 0845 756 7765

British Exporters Association, Broadway House, Tothill Street, London SW1H 9NQ; Tel: 020 7222 5419 (www.bexa.co.uk)

Companies Registration Office, Companies House, Crown Way, Cardiff CF14 3UZ; Tel: 029 2038 8588 (www.companies-house.co.uk)

Data Protection Registrar, Wycliffe House, Water Lane, Wilmslow, Cheshire SK9 5AF; Tel: 01625 545700 (www.open.gov.uk/dpr/drphome.htm)

Direct Marketing Association (has details of events, news releases, industry standards, case histories), Haymarket House, 1 Oxendon Street, London SW1Y 4EE; Tel: 020 7321 2525 (www.dma.org.uk)

European Information Centres (provides SMEs with information on European issues); Tel: 020 7489 1992 (London) (www.londonchamber.co.uk or www.euro-info.org.uk)

Equal Opportunities Commission, Arndale House, Arndale Centre, Manchester M4 3EQ; Tel: 0161 833 9244 (www.eoc.org.uk)

Export Market Information Centre (public library of overseas market intelligence, open Mon–Thurs 9 a.m.–8 p.m., Fri 9 a.m.–5.30 p.m.), Kingsgate House, 66–74 Victoria Street, London SW1E 6SW; Tel: 020 7215 5444

Federation of Small Businesses (small business lobby group in the UK; website has online directories, news and press releases), Whittle Way, Blackpool Business Park, Blackpool, Lancashire FY4 2FE; Tel: 01253 336000 (www.fsb.org.uk)

Growth Company Investor (includes financial reports, news and archive on AIM and OFEX listed companies), 9 Harley Street, London W1N 1DA; Tel: 020 7323 4050 (www.growthcompany.co.uk)

Inland Revenue's New Employers Helpline (provides information for new employers on PAYE, matters of pay and general queries); Tel: 0845 607 0143 (weekdays 8 a.m.–8 p.m., Sat/Sun 8 a.m.–5 p.m.)

Institute of Patentees and Inventors (gives advice on all aspects of inventing), Suite 505a, Triumph House, 189 Regent Street, London W1B 4JY; Tel: 020 7434 1818 (www.invent.org.uk)

Institute of Business Advisers (non-profit-making institute of advisers, mentors and trainers who specialise in helping small businesses);

membership address: PO Box 8, Harrogate, North Yorkshire HG2 8XB; Tel: 01423 879208 (www.iba.org.uk)

Market Research Society, 15 Northburgh Street, London EC1V 0JR; Tel: 020 7490 4911 (www.mrs.org.uk)

National Business Angels Network (provides a matching service to investors, also publishes profiles of new businesses in magazine), 40–42 Cannon Street, London EC4N 6JJ; Tel: 020 7329 2929 (www.bestmatch.co.uk)

National Federation of Enterprise Agencies (represents local enterprise agencies and does its own research projects), Trinity Gardens, 9–11 Bromham Road, Bedford MK40 2UQ; Tel: 01234 354055 (www.nfea.com)

Nominet UK (registers internet domain names), Sandford Gate, Sandy Lane West, Oxford OX4 6LB; Tel: 01865 332211 (www.nominet.org.uk)

OneLondon Business Angels (business angel network), c/o Greater London Enterprise, 28 Park Street, London SE1 9EQ; Tel: 020 7940 1547 (www.businessangels-london.co.uk)

The Patent Office, Concept House, Cardiff Road, Newport, South Wales NP10 8QQ; Tel: 01633 814000 (www.patent.gov.uk)

The Prince's Trust (offers low-interest loans and advice from mentors etc. to 18–30 year olds), 18 Park Square East, London NW1 4LH; Tel: 020 7543 1234 (www.princes-trust.org.uk)

Recruitment and Employment Confederation (website includes events, news and advice), 36–38 Mortimer Street, London W1N 7RB; Tel: 020 762 3260 (www.rec.uk.com)

Shell LiveWIRE (offers useful links, 'essential business kit' and competition; open to 16–30 year old entrepreneurs); Tel: 0845 7573252 (www.shell-livewire.org)

Small Firms Loan Guarantee Scheme; Tel: 0114 2597308/9, Fax: 0114 2597316, email: sflgs@sbs.gsi.gov.uk (www.sbs.gov.uk/SFLGS)

You may also find some of the other books available in this series useful. For example, *The Bottom Line* by Paul Barrow and *Kick-Start Your Business* by Robert Craven.

Aardman: David Sproxton and Peter Lord
Sproxton and Lord, both born in the mid-fifties, established their company, Aardman, in 1973, and had their first big hit with the animated television character Morph. In 1986 they recruited film student Nick Park and in 2000 produced the film *Chicken Run* with the US studio DreamWorks.

Agency.com: Eamonn Wilmott and Andy Hobsbawm
Hobsbawm played guitar in a rock band before, at the age of 27, answering an 'entrepreneur wanted' advert. Wilmott founded Internet Publishing in 1994 and teamed up with Hobsbawm shortly afterwards; they created Online Magic a year later. In 1998 they sold their business to Agency.com, and now run Agency's operations in Europe.

Alchemy Partners: Jon Moulton
Moulton ran Schroder Ventures in the eighties and left in the early nineties to work for another venture firm, Apax. In 1997 he decided to set up his own venture capital business.

Angela Mortimer: Angela and John Mortimer
The Mortimers met in the seventies and shared a flat: she was a former teacher-turned-secretary; he was a salesman selling vacuum cleaners. In 1976 the couple set up their own secretarial recruitment consultancy, and it is now an international enterprise employing more than 300 people. They also have two children.

Anne Storey: Anne Storey and Robert Eitel
Storey was introduced to Eitel by her former tutor at the Royal College of Art. She was working for Nicole Farhi; he was running the Paul Costelloe label. They launched their own label in 1997.

ATTIK: Simon Needham and James Sommerville
Both born in 1966, the pair met at art college and in 1986 launched their graphic design business in Huddersfield with a £1,000 grant from the Prince's Trust. They have turned it into a design consultancy with studios around the world.

Avalon: Jon Thoday and Richard Allen-Turner
Allen-Turner was a student entertainments officer when Thoday, a promoter, hired him in the eighties. The pair went on to sign famous names to their management agency, including Rob Newman and David Baddiel in the early nineties. Their group now includes publicity and television arms.

Brainspark: Stewart Dodd
Dodd worked for various banks in the City for seventeen years before leaving in 1999 to launch an incubator venture, Brainspark.

Carroll and Brown: Amy Carroll
Carroll arrived in London from the States in the mid-seventies and began working as a typist at publisher Dorling Kindersley. She became editorial director there, before leaving with Denise Brown in 1989 to form a book packaging and publishing company.

Cavendish Corporate Finance: Howard Leigh
Born in the late fifties, Leigh and his partner, Hugo Haddon-Grant, worked as chartered accountants before setting up a corporate finance boutique in 1988 to provide a service to vendors of businesses.

Charlotte Productions: Charlotte Barker
Barker grew up in Dundee and went to college in the mid-eighties to train as a social worker. While there, she designed her own 'ice-breaker' board game and, in the late nineties, began to develop it as a commercial enterprise under the brand name Vamos.

Charlton House: Robyn Jones
Robyn Jones was a senior executive in a large contract catering company but in 1991, when she was made redundant, she decided to set up her own contract-catering business from home in Oxfordshire. Her husband Tim, an accountant, later joined the business full time.

City Industrial Group: Jack Morris
Morris, the youngest of five brothers, worked in a shoe shop and trained in accounts before becoming deputy chairman and then chairman of the business founded by his father in 1954. In the eighties the group acquired the Business Design Centre in London.

CKD Kennedy Macpherson: Jon Kennedy and Andrew Macpherson
Kennedy grew up on an estate his father managed in Scotland and studied land management at university. In 1992 he set up Clegg Kennedy Drew with two partners; Macpherson, a partner at the agency Knight Frank, joined him some eighteen months later.

Clear Channel: Roger Parry
Clear Channel Communications is one of the world's largest out-of-home media groups. Parry, born in 1953 and based in London, is responsible for operations in Europe, Asia and Africa. He was previously chief executive of More Group, a European company acquired by Clear Channel. Before that, he was development director of Aegis Group, and formerly a journalist, producer and management consultant.

Conchango plc: Mike Altendorf and Richard Thwaite
Altendorf and Thwaite met at university in the early eighties. The pair worked for a systems integration start-up firm that folded in 1988, and then decided to launch their own IT consultancy.

Countryside Properties: Graham and Richard Cherry
Graham joined his father Alan's business, Countryside, in 1980 as its first graduate trainee; Richard, two years younger, followed soon after. Graham is now chief executive and Richard director of new business.

The Curtain Exchange: Juliana Galvin and Liz Meston

Galvin, formerly a nurse, and Meston, who had worked in the rag trade, met at a lunch party when they were both young mothers. In 1990 the pair opened their first shop in Suffolk and, after six months, opened the first of several more shops, this time in Fulham. Their range now includes ready-made and bespoke curtains.

Dataworkforce: Neil Franklin

Franklin, born in 1964, became a door-to-door salesman at the age of eighteen. He worked for a kitchens company before becoming a recruitment consultant and moving into IT recruitment. In 1991 he started his own business from his front room in Bromley, starting in IT and communications recruitment and moving into telecoms. By 2000, his was one of the fastest-growing companies in the UK.

Deep Water Recovery and Exploration: Moya and Alec Crawford

Moya Crawford met her diver husband Alec as he worked to salvage a shipwreck off the Scottish island of Foula in 1973. The pair have run their own salvage company for nearly twenty years and more recently set up a marine technology business called Deep Tek.

Domino's Pizza: Colin Halpern

Halpern was born in 1937 and trained at night school to become an engineer. He borrowed £5,000 to start his first business in the States in his early thirties, and went on to establish a number of different businesses, including a successful car rental franchise in New York City. In 1993, he bought the UK master franchise for an American pizza chain, Domino's Pizza.

Easyscreen: Philip Docker and Paul Varcoe

Varcoe worked his way up to become head options trader for Salomon Brothers before going solo as a 'local' trader. Docker's father owned a fruit and vegetable business; Philip Docker went into trading futures on the London International Financial Futures and Options Exchange (LIFFE). The pair left LIFFE in the late nineties to develop software systems for traders.

Energy Power Resources: David Williams and Malcolm Chilton
Williams bought his first briefcase at the age of thirteen. He sold video games at college, then trained as an engineer and worked for South West Electricity Company (SWALEC) until 1996. He left to join EPR, a shell firm financing renewable energy projects. Chilton, a partner from an earlier joint venture, joined him and the pair have since established several leading renewable energy projects.

EuroRSCG Wnek Gosper: Brett Gosper
In 1994 Mark Wnek, a copywriter, became head of the advertising agency EuroRSCG in London. He persuaded Gosper, deputy managing director of one of France's leading agencies, to join him as co-head of the agency.

Filtronic: Chris Snowden and David Rhodes
Rhodes was a lecturer at Leeds University in 1974, where Snowden was an undergraduate. Three years later, Rhodes set up Filtronic, taking on his first employees in 1979. For ten years, the company made components for electronic warfare then began to work in mobile telephony. Snowden, who ran a department at Leeds, joined Filtronic in 1997.

FirstMark: Lynn Forester and Michael Price
Forester trained as a lawyer and acquired mobile phone companies for Metromedia in the eighties. She then bought her own telecoms business. Later Price, who worked for Lazard Freres, helped her to sell the business and she offered him a stake in her new broadband Internet venture. In 2000 the pair raised more than $1bn to finance their pan-European network.

The Food Ferry: James Millar and Jonathan Hartnell-Beavis
Millar was a lawyer at the City firm Freshfields until his friend Hartnell-Beavis, a builder, suggested they start up a grocery home-shopping service together. In 1990 Millar borrowed £10,000 from his father and the pair launched The Food Ferry in London.

Forward Publishing: Neil Mendoza and William Sieghart
Mendoza and Sieghart met at Oxford in the late seventies and started their publishing agency in 1986.

FrameStore: William Sargent and Sharon Reed

Sargent and Reed met in 1982. Reed, whose family ran an antiques business, worked for Robert Maxwell's British Printing and Communications Corporation before founding FrameStore in 1986 with Sargent, the executive producer of television's *Spitting Image*. They acquired the Computer Film Company in 1997 and in 2000 produced the hit series *Walking with Dinosaurs* with the BBC. They are married and have two children.

Future Forests: Dan Morrell and Sue Welland

Morrell was an agent and Welland worked for a PR firm when the pair met in the eighties. In 1995, they started Future Forests based on Morrell's 'trees idea' – planting trees on behalf of companies and individuals to offset carbon dioxide emissions.

The Gadget Shop: Jon Elvidge and Andrew Hobbs

In 1991 Elvidge, a salesman for Kingston Communications, persuaded Hobbs, a property developer, to assign him a retail unit in a new shopping centre in Hull. He opened The Gadget Shop, and Hobbs later paid £25,000 to buy half the company and became his business partner.

Gullane Entertainment plc: Charles Falzon and William Harris

Harris, an accountant, joined Britt Allcroft in 1986 shortly after she bought the rights to *Thomas the Tank Engine*. In the early nineties he produced a television series in the States with Falzon, who later joined the board and became group president, with Harris as chief executive.

Haymarket: Simon Tindall and Michael Heseltine

Tindall met Heseltine in 1959 when he was hired to sell advertising space for what became Haymarket. The pair have worked together periodically for more than forty years.

Helphire plc: Mark Jackson and Michael Symons

Symons 'made a lot of money out of law and lost it in property' before he joined his squash partner Jackson to start up Helphire. Their idea was for a credit hire business to arrange car repairs, insurance payouts and vehicle replacements for accident victims. The company was founded in 1992 and floated in 1997.

Home House: Brian Clivaz and Richard Farleigh
In 1996 Clivaz left his job as managing director of the London restaurant Simpson's-in-the-Strand to found a private members club with Farleigh, formerly a hedge fund manager. The pair raised £12m to restore Home House, a Grade I listed building north of Oxford Street.

Hotel du Vin: Robin Hutson and Gerard Basset
Basset, born in France, came to England to work as a dishwasher after watching his football team play at Liverpool. Hutson, the general manager of a leading country hotel, hired him in 1988 as his sommelier. Six years later, the pair raised £1.25m to open their first hotel in Winchester, and have since opened several more hotels together.

Ideal World: Zad Rogers and Hamish Barbour
Rogers, a television producer, met the presenter Muriel Gray in the eighties and joined her and her partner Barbour in making a series about fictional artists. When, in the nineties, Gray stepped back to concentrate on writing fiction, Barbour and Rogers became partners.

iMPOWER: Heather Rabbatts and Alasdair Liddell
Rabbatts was the chief executive of Lambeth Council before launching her venture, in March 2000, providing online services for local and national government departments. Liddell was director of planning at the NHS.

Improveline: Marshall King
Born in 1966, King studied maths before becoming a management consultant. In early 1999 he left Dun & Bradstreet to found a service sourcing home decorators and builders, for which he raised £11m in venture capital funding.

Innocent: Richard Reed, Jon Wright and Adam Balon
All born in the early seventies, Reed, Wright and Balon met as undergraduates at Cambridge and left to work in marketing, advertising and consultancy. Four years after graduating, they began to develop 'smoothie' fruit juices, and now sell to thousands of outlets in the UK from their London headquarters, Fruit Towers.

Internet Business Group: Maziar Darvish
Born in 1975, Darvish wrote computer games as a teenager and set up his first company Mazware.com a month after graduation. He later incorporated it into his Internet Business Group, which floated on the Alternative Investment Market in 2000.

Iron Bed Company: Simon and Anne Notley
The Notleys met in the seventies on a flotilla in Corfu. They ran a windsurfing school before moving into selling stripped pine furniture, but were led to the verge of bankruptcy by a misconceived venture in futon-style beds. In 1995 they set up the Iron Bed Company, one of the UK's fastest-growing businesses.

John Frieda: John Frieda and Gail Federici
Frieda followed his father and grandfather into hairdressing, opening his own salon at the age of 25. He began selling products to the UK pharmacy chain Boots, and then met Federici, the vice-president of a large American products company, who joined him as a business partner.

King of Shaves: Will King and Herbie Dayal
Born in 1965, King worked for a conference firm before being made redundant in 1991. With the help of his wife and Dayal, a former management consultant, King set up a business making shaving products. The brand has since expanded into Europe and the US.

Le Maitre: Karen Haddon
Haddon was a singer and actress before joining the business established by her father, Harold Berlinski. She started as a secretary and worked her way up to manage the group's fireworks division.

Liontrust: Nigel Legge and William Carey
Legge and Carey worked together in the mid-eighties and moved together to the stockbroker James Capel. In 1994 they established their own unit trust company, now known as Liontrust.

Listawood: Arthur and Irene Allen
Allen, a maths teacher, and his wife Irene, a biochemist, borrowed money from their family in 1987 to set up a business in a rural

Norfolk town producing magnetic games and promotional gifts. Their company is now a leading producer of computer mouse mats.

Livingstone Guarantee: Barrie Pearson

Born in 1939, Pearson worked in mergers and acquisitions for large companies before launching his corporate finance boutique in 1976.

Loot: David Landau

Landau set up his free-ads operation with his brother-in-law in 1984 after being inspired by a newspaper he saw abroad. An art historian by training, he grew the business into an international operation before selling it to Scoot in September 2000.

Lush: Mark Constantine and Andrew Gerrie

Constantine met Anita Roddick while he was in his early twenties, and became one of the biggest suppliers to The Body Shop. In the eighties he founded Cosmetics to Go, which later collapsed. In the mid-nineties he and Gerrie, a property dealer, launched the cosmetics brand Lush, and have since opened shops around the world.

The Media Vehicle: Jessica Hatfield

Jessica Hatfield, now in her forties, left school at seventeen to set up her first business, in catering. She worked in sales promotion and business development for several companies before launching her own business The Media Vehicle in 1995, providing clients with 'ambient media' coverage.

Ncipher plc: Alex and Nicko van Someren

As a teenager Alex worked for the Cambridge computer firm Acorn with his brother Nicko. Later, they started running companies together and were offered money by a Canadian venture capital firm to start a company making encryption products, Ncipher. In 2000 they floated it on the main stock exchange in London.

Orchestream, i-Gabriel, Interprovider: Charlie Muirhead

Muirhead did his first management buyout at the age of eighteen. He went to study at Imperial College but left early to start his own technology company, Orchestream, in 1996. Three years later, he moved into a non-executive role when he hired Ashley Ward as chief executive. He then went on to start up a business angel network, i-Gabriel, and has since been working on a new project, Interprovider.

The Partners: David Stuart and Aziz Cami

Stuart and Cami trained as designers and shared an art studio in Shoreditch in the eighties. They began winning design awards and grew their business throughout the nineties. In 2000, The Partners was bought by Young & Rubicam, now part of the advertising group WPP.

Partners for Change: Tim Connolly and Mark Smith

Connolly's first experience of enterprise was to set up a football club at the age of fourteen. He met Smith at the accountancy firm KPMG in the late eighties. In 1994 they left to set up their own business change consultancy.

Perfunktory Group: Scott Lyons

Lyons was born in the early seventies and studied in Florida before joining MTV as a marketing executive. He left in 1996 to found his digital and new media Perfunktory Group in New York City with two friends. They later moved to London.

The Perfume Shop: Philip Newton and Jeremy Seigal

Newton started his first business at the age of 22. Through an investor, he got to know Seigal's father; twenty years later he began working with Seigal at the Merchant Retail Group. They bought a failing business, Ozone, renamed it The Perfume Shop and have since rolled out the brand around the UK.

Poptones: Alan McGee and Julian Richer

At nineteen, Richer started Richer Sounds, the first in a line of businesses. McGee co-founded the record label Creation in the eighties. The pair met at a dinner party in 1999 and, in 2000, floated their record label Poptones on the Alternative Investment Market.

Punch Group: Roger Myers

Roger Myers was born in 1947 and trained as an accountant. He worked in the music business before leaving to open his first cocktail bar, Peppermint Park, in the late seventies, in a former car showroom near Leicester Square. He co-founded the restaurant and bar chains Café Rouge and Dôme and in 1997 started the pubs group Punch with Hugh Osmond, the entrepreneur behind PizzaExpress.

Rees Pollock: Simon Rees and Andrew Pollock

Pollock met Rees when they were both partners at Ernst & Young, running a division advising small businesses. In 1989 they left with two others to set up 'a big firm in a small box' – an accountancy practice providing advice and services to small businesses.

Regus: Mark Dixon

Born in 1959 to an engineer and a secretary, Dixon left school in Chelmsford with a clutch of O-Levels and rose to be one of Britain's most successful entrepreneurs. He used profits from other businesses to start up Regus in 1989, now a global network of business centres.

Revise.it: Nick Rose and Jordan Mayo

Rose and Mayo met as pupils at Manchester Grammar School and went on to study at Oxford University in 1999. At sixteen, they set up a company to publish revision guides, later bought by Oxford University Press. They then started one of the UK's leading revision websites.

Revolution: Roy Ellis and Neil Macleod

Employed in the leisure industry, Ellis and Macleod met socially and began to open city-style bars on the outskirts of cities in the early nineties. In 1996, they developed the Revolution 'vodka bar' concept.

River Publishing: Nicola Murphy and Jane Wynn

Murphy spent six years working for Procter & Gamble after university then joined The Publishing Team, but left with Wynn to start her own publishing venture in 1994.

St Luke's: David Abraham and Andy Law

Abraham joined the US advertising agency Benton & Bowles in the early eighties and met Law in 1987. Both moved to Chiat/Day, and in 1995 took their team to form a new agency, called St Luke's. Abraham left in spring 2001 to join the television group Discovery.

Select-a-Skip: James Keay

Keay, a business studies graduate, initially worked three evenings a week at Little Chef to fund the business he started in his bedroom. Born in the early seventies, he founded his company in 1996 after working for a waste disposal company for six months. He took on his first employee after four months and now has a network of sub-contractors serving thousands of customers. In 2000, he was a finalist in the Shell LiveWIRE competition.

Seymour Powell: Richard Seymour and Dick Powell

Both halves of the partnership trained at the Royal College of Art but only met later "in the supplies cupboard at St Albans" where both were working as lecturers. From the early eighties they shared an office, and have since built a reputation as two of the UK's leading industrial designers.

Shawn Taylor Racing: Shawn Taylor

Taylor was born in 1971 and developed a passion for racing as a teenager. In his twenties he studied engineering and business management and in 1999 started a service centre in a Norfolk village, with the long-term aim of establishing his own racing team. He was a finalist in Shell LiveWIRE's 2001 competition.

Alex Shipp

Shipp studied computer science at Cambridge and set up his own software company in the mid nineties. He then joined Star Technology as an anti-virus technologist.

ShopSmart: Daniel and Leo Gestetner

The Gestetners, great-grandsons of the inventor of the first photocopier, founded ShopSmart in 1998 as a shopping portal which allowed consumers to compare prices. They sold it in 2001.

Sibelius: Ben and Jonathan Finn

The Finns decided as teenagers to write the world's best computer software for music composers and publishers. Their Sibelius software is now used by leading musicians and the group they founded in 1993 is a global leader in music notation software.

Silicon Media Group: Anna Russell and Rob Lewis
Russell and Lewis founded the business and IT news operation Silicon.com in 1997. Their site operates out of offices and studios in Chelsea, Munich and Paris. The pair met after studying at Cambridge.

Smarterwork: Jan Van den Berghe
Van den Berghe was educated in Belgium and moved to Zurich to work for the Boston Consulting Group. In 1999 he and two co-founders raised $1m seed capital and set up headquarters in London, offering a managed marketplace for business services. They secured second round funding of $12m from European venture capitalists and launched the full service in early 2000.

Somethin' Else: Jez Nelson and Sonita Alleyne
Nelson and Alleyne, both born in the mid-sixties, met while working at the radio station JazzFM. They left in 1991 to start their own business and one of their earliest productions was Festival FM, a radio station for the Edinburgh Festival. They now run one of Britain's leading independent radio production companies.

Sophos: Jan Hruska and Peter Lammer
Hruska and Lammer, born in the late fifties, met as post-graduate students at Oxford and developed their own laptop computer. They went on to start Sophos in 1985, based in Abingdon. Their anti-virus products now protect many FTSE 100 companies.

Speed plc: Martin Rutty and Tim Gilbert
Collecting coins as a child gave Rutty 'an idea about money' and his first enterprise was to sell a pair of flippers to his brother for 50 pence. After three weeks at university, he left to work for a courier firm and his friend Gilbert soon joined him to found Speed in 1978.

Synthetic Dimensions: Kate Copestake and Kevin Bulmer
Copestake was an industrial designer before founding an animation company with her domestic partner, Bulmer, also a designer, in 1985. In 2000 they listed their company on the trading facility OFEX.

Ten Rooms: Terry Pullen
Pullen, born in 1965, was in his twenties when, while convalescing from an accident, he developed plans for his first restaurant. Later, he ran a wine bar and a financial services company before raising money in the late nineties to establish city bars in central London.

ThinkNatural: Carol Dukes and Emma Crowe
Carol Dukes left Oxford in 1984 to join a small company developing satellite television. Six years later she did an MBA at London Business School before joining emap in 1993 to establish its online operation. She then moved to Carlton, where she met Crowe, who had worked for AOL and in 1999 the pair started their natural health venture.

Topps Tiles plc: Barry Bester and Stuart Williams
Bester took his first profit-share at the age of twenty and then ran a hairdressing business with his wife, before joining Williams to buy a small tile shop in west London in the early eighties. They opened more shops and, in 1986, teamed up with another tile retailer, Ted Derbyshire. In 1997 they floated the business on the London stock exchange.

The Union: Simon Scott and Andrew Lindsay
Scott and Lindsay met at Hall's advertising agency in Edinburgh in the eighties and worked together as creative directors at a newly formed agency, Faulds, before leaving in 1996 to found their own agency.

United Designers: Keith Hobbs and Linzi Coppick
Hobbs and Coppick designed restaurants for Sir Terence Conran before branching out on their own with three others in 1994.

Vivid Imaginations: Nick Austin and Alan Bennie
Austin worked for Procter & Gamble before moving to the toy maker Matchbox, where he met Bennie. When Matchbox was sold in 1992, they left to start up Vivid, which, in eight years, has built a turnover of £74m.

Yeoman Group plc: Hugh Agnew and Charles Marshall
Agnew, born in 1950, met Marshall at Cambridge before going on to

work in the nascent offshore industry and to develop navigation technology for yacht products. In the early nineties he asked Marshall to help him launch the technology for consumer use. Their company was AIM's top performer in 2000.

Zeus Technology: Adam Twiss and Damian Reeves

Twiss was born in 1976 and studied with Reeves at Cambridge, where they developed web server technology in their spare hours. When they left in 1997, they established a company that soon became one of Cambridge's fastest growing start-ups, and completed three rounds of funding worth $13 million.

ZTT: Trevor Horn and Jill Sinclair

Horn, a bass guitarist, recorded in Sinclair's brother's studio in 1977. She failed to sign up his first record 'Video Killed The Radio Star', but they started going out, got married and began to build their record company ZTT. Horn went on to produce albums for Seal and the Art of Noise.

Index

(Bold indicates the name of the main company as given in the Who's Who, pages 173–87)